Scaffolding for Success

Support and scaffolding are critical for moving students to higher levels of learning. But how do we ensure we're giving the "right" work and not just *extra* work? Barbara R. Blackburn has the answers in this important new book. She provides a plethora of strategies for helping students create meaning and become more independent so they can truly learn at rigorous levels.

First, she examines the basics of rigor and scaffolding and uncovers the role of planning in scaffolding, including the difference between acceleration and remediation and examples of differentiating instruction with scaffolding. Then she demonstrates a variety of ways to add scaffolding into classroom discourse, vocabulary, comprehension, and writing across the curriculum. Ideas and strategies are provided for different subject areas and levels, so you can easily apply them to your own setting. And finally, she shows the roles of formative assessment and social emotional learning in scaffolding.

With this practical book, you'll have a toolkit of great ideas at your disposal as you foster a learning environment of high expectations and success.

Dr. Barbara R. Blackburn, a Top 30 Global Guru in Education, is the bestselling author of over 30 books and is a sought-after national and international consultant. She was an award-winning professor at Winthrop University and has taught early childhood, elementary, middle, and high school students.

Melissa Miles is a middle school language arts teacher. Previously, she was Director of Educational Resources at a school in North Carolina. She has 25 years of classroom teaching experience. She is also twice credentialed as a National Board-Certified teacher, works as a SpringBoard Curriculum consultant to College Board, and is a certified member of the site visitation team for the Schools to Watch award.

Also Available from BARBARA R. BLACKBURN
(www.routledge.com/k-12)

**Rigor in the 6–12 ELA and Social Studies Classroom:
A Teacher Toolkit**
Barbara R. Blackburn and Melissa Miles

**Rigor in the K-5 ELA and Social Studies Classroom:
A Teacher Toolkit**
Barbara R. Blackburn and Melissa Miles

**Rigor in the K-5 Math and Science Classroom:
A Teacher Toolkit**
Barbara R. Blackburn and Abbigail Armstrong

**Rigor in the 6–12 Math and Science Classroom:
A Teacher Toolkit**
Barbara R. Blackburn and Abbigail Armstrong

**Rigor in the RTI and MTSS Classroom:
Practical Tools and Strategies**
Barbara R. Blackburn and Bradley S. Witzel

Rigor and Assessment in the Classroom
Barbara R. Blackburn

**Motivating Struggling Learners:
10 Ways to Build Student Success**
Barbara R. Blackburn

Rigor for Students with Special Needs, 2e
Barbara R. Blackburn and Bradley Witzel

Rigor Made Easy: Getting Started
Barbara R. Blackburn

Rigor in Your School: A Toolkit for Leaders
Ronald Williamson and Barbara R. Blackburn

**Rigor in the Remote Learning Classroom:
Instructional Tips and Strategies**
Barbara R. Blackburn

Scaffolding for Success

Helping Learners Meet Rigorous Expectations Across the Curriculum

Barbara R. Blackburn with
Melissa Miles

Routledge
Taylor & Francis Group
NEW YORK AND LONDON

Designed cover image: Getty Images

First published 2025
by Routledge
605 Third Avenue, New York, NY 10158

and by Routledge
4 Park Square, Milton Park, Abingdon, Oxon, OX14 4RN

Routledge is an imprint of the Taylor & Francis Group, an informa business

© 2025 Barbara R. Blackburn

The right of Barbara R. Blackburn to be identified as author of this work has been asserted in accordance with sections 77 and 78 of the Copyright, Designs and Patents Act 1988.

All rights reserved. The purchase of this copyright material confers the right on the purchasing institution to photocopy or download pages which bear a copyright line at the bottom of the page. No other parts of this book may be reprinted or reproduced or utilised in any form or by any electronic, mechanical, or other means, now known or hereafter invented, including photocopying and recording, or in any information storage or retrieval system, without permission in writing from the publishers.

Trademark notice: Product or corporate names may be trademarks or registered trademarks, and are used only for identification and explanation without intent to infringe.

ISBN: 978-1-032-82834-3 (hbk)
ISBN: 978-1-032-71054-9 (pbk)
ISBN: 978-1-003-50656-0 (ebk)

DOI: 10.4324/9781003506560

Typeset in Palatino
by Apex CoVantage, LLC

Access the Support Material: www.routledge.com/9781032710549

Support Material

The following tools from the book are also available on our website as free downloads, so you can easily print and reproduce them for classroom use. To access the materials, go to the book product page at www.routledge.com/9781032710549 and click on the link that says Support Material.

Cooperative Learning Rubrics (Simple and Complex)
Vocabulary Graphic Organizer
Flesh It Out ELA
Flesh It Out Social Studies
Flesh It Out Math
Flesh It Out Science
Fishbone
Graphic Organizer for Debates
Pizza Wheel
Decision Tree Template
Cubing Pattern

Dedication

To My Best Friend and Sister, Abbigail Armstrong,
who unexpectedly died in 2023. I watched you grow from
a former student into a co-author, or as you would say, from a
caterpillar into a butterfly. I miss you every day. We were
to write this book together, and I hope I incorporated your
spirit in a way that honors you. —*Barbara*

This book is dedicated to my three beautiful children.
May they always be driven to learn and curious
about the world around them. —*Missy*

Contents

Acknowledgements xi
Meet the Authors xiii

1 **Rigor and Scaffolding** 1

2 **Planning for Scaffolding Instruction** 9

3 **Scaffolding Classroom Discourse** 21

4 **Scaffolding Vocabulary Throughout the Curriculum** 53

5 **Scaffolding Comprehension Across the Subject Areas** 77

6 **Scaffolding Writing in the Content Areas** 105

7 **Formative Assessment Supports Scaffolding** 133

8 **Social and Emotional Skills for Scaffolding** 147

9 **Common Concerns About Scaffolding** 163

   Bibliography 177

Acknowledgements

A special thank you to Melissa Miles, who helped me throughout the book, adding examples and insight.

For my husband, Pete, who is my constant support and encouragement.

For my mother, who, at 90, continues to teach and encourage me.

As always, to Lauren Davis, my editor, publisher, and friend. As always, I could not have done this without you.

To Emma Capel, thank you for a wonderful cover design.

To Apex CoVantage for all the work coordinating production, and a special thank you to Autumn Spalding who always makes the production process easy.

Finally, for all the teachers and leaders I work with, you continue to inspire me daily. I'd like to especially thank Graham Local Schools in Ohio and Clark Public Schools in New Jersey for their collaborations. —*Barbara*

Barbara Blackburn—your belief in me is greatly appreciated. Thank you for pushing me to try new things and expand my horizons.

The faculty and staff at Charlotte Christian School—thank you for pushing educators to think beyond the obvious and connect with students on a level that helps them to grow academically, emotionally, socially, and spiritually.

My husband—your patience, love, and understanding exceed what I deserve. —*Missy*

Meet the Authors

Dr. Barbara R. Blackburn, an international speaker and Top 30 Global Guru, has dedicated her life to raising the level of rigor and motivation for professional educators and students alike. What differentiates Barbara's over 30 books are her easily executable, concrete examples based on decades of experience as a teacher, professor, and consultant. Barbara's dedication to education was inspired in her early years by her parents. Her father's doctorate and lifetime career as a professor taught her the importance of professional training. Her mother's career as school secretary shaped Barbara's appreciation of the effort all staff play in the education of every child.

Barbara has taught early childhood, elementary, middle, and high school students and has served as an educational consultant for three publishing companies. She holds a master's degree in School Administration and was certified as both a teacher and school principal in North Carolina. She received her Ph.D. in Curriculum and Teaching from the University of North Carolina at Greensboro. In 2006, she received the award for Outstanding Junior Professor at Winthrop University. She left her position at the University of North Carolina at Charlotte to write and speak full-time. She was recently appointed Judge as part of The Educator 2024 Education Awards, the leading independent awards event across the K12 sector for Australia and New Zealand.

In addition to speaking at state, national, and international conferences, she also regularly presents workshops for teachers and administrators in elementary, middle, and high schools, both remotely and on-site. Her workshops are lively and engaging and filled with practical information. Her most popular topics include:

- Rigor is NOT a Four-Letter Word
- Rigorous Schools and Classrooms: Leading the Way
- Motivation + Engagement + Rigor = Student Success
- Rigor for Students with Special Needs
- Instructional Strategies that Motivate Students
- Scaffolding Strategies for the Young and the Restless
- Motivating Yourself and Others
- Engaging Instruction Leads to Higher Achievement
- High Expectations and Increased Support Lead to Success

Melissa Miles is currently back in the classroom teaching middle school language arts after serving as Director of Educational Resources at a school in Charlotte, North Carolina. She has 25 years of classroom teaching experience. She is also twice credentialed as a National Board-Certified teacher for young adolescents, works as a SpringBoard Curriculum consultant to College Board, and is a certified member of the site visitation team for the Schools to Watch award. She is coauthor of *Rigor in the 6–12 ELA and Social Studies Classroom*, *Rigor in the K–5 ELA and Social Studies Classroom*, and *Rigor in the Remote Learning Classroom* with Barbara R. Blackburn.

1
Rigor and Scaffolding

Instructional rigor is a key component of effective instruction. Too often, we think that our instruction is rigorous, but oftentimes, it is not. Our assumptions about rigor as well as our practices make a difference in what we expect from students. One of the biggest misconceptions about rigor is that scaffolding should not be a part of rigor. In fact, scaffolding is a core part of rigorous instruction. The higher the level of rigor, the higher the need for support.

Many of you have read some of my other books or heard me speak, so the first part of this chapter will serve as a review. In this chapter, we'll quickly look at the full definition of rigor, then focus on the role scaffolding plays in rigorous instruction.

Defining Rigor

Now that we have looked at what rigor is *not*, let's look at what rigor *is*. In *Rigor is Not a Four Letter Word*, I define rigor as: Creating an environment in which:

- each student is expected to learn at high levels;
- each student is supported so he or she can learn at high levels;
- each student demonstrates learning at high levels.

Notice we are looking at the environment you create. The tri-fold approach to rigor is not limited to the curriculum students are expected to learn. It is more than a specific lesson or instructional strategy. It is deeper than what a student says or does in response to a lesson. True rigor is the result of weaving together all elements of schooling to raise students to higher levels of learning. Let's take a deeper look at the three aspects of the definition.

Expecting Students to Learn at High Levels

The first component of rigor is creating an environment in which each student is expected to learn at high levels. Having high expectations starts with the recognition that every student possesses the potential to succeed at his or her individual level.

Almost every teacher or leader I talk with says, "We have high expectations for our students." Sometimes, that is evidenced by the behaviors in the school; other times, however, faculty actions don't match the words. There are concrete ways to implement and assess rigor in classrooms.

As you design lessons that incorporate more rigorous opportunities for learning, you will want to consider the questions that are embedded in the instruction. Higher-level questioning is an integral part of a rigorous classroom. Look for open-ended questions—ones that are at higher levels. You'll find more on questioning in Chapter 3.

It is also important to pay attention to how you respond to student questions. When we visit schools, it is not uncommon to see teachers who ask higher-level questions. But for whatever reason, I then see some of the same teachers accept low-level responses from students. In rigorous classrooms, teachers push students to respond at high levels. They ask extending questions. Extending questions are questions that encourage a student to explain their reasoning and think through ideas. When a student does not know the immediate answer but has sufficient background information to provide a response to the question, the teacher continues to probe and guide the student's thinking rather than moving on to the next student. Insist on thinking and problem solving.

Supporting Students to Learn at High Levels

High expectations are important, but the most rigorous schools ensure that each student is supported so he or she can learn at high levels, which is the second part of our definition. It is essential that teachers design lessons that move students to more challenging work while simultaneously providing ongoing scaffolding to support students' learning as they move to those higher levels.

Providing additional scaffolding throughout lessons is one of the most important ways to support your students. Oftentimes, students have the ability or knowledge to accomplish a task but are overwhelmed at the complexity of it, therefore getting lost in the process. This can occur in a variety of ways, but it requires that teachers ask themselves during every step of their lessons, "What extra support might my students need?" This is the focus of this book.

Ensuring Students Demonstrate Learning at High Levels

The third component of a rigorous classroom is providing each student with opportunities to demonstrate learning at high levels. A teacher recently said to me, "If we provide more challenging lessons that include extra support, then learning will happen." What I've learned is that if we want students to show us they understand what they learned at a high level, we also need to provide opportunities for students to demonstrate they have truly mastered that learning. In order for students to demonstrate their learning, they must first be engaged in academic tasks—precisely, those in the classroom.

Student engagement is a critical aspect of rigor. In too many classrooms, most of the instruction consists of the teacher-centered, large-group instruction, perhaps in an interactive lecture or discussion format. The general practice during these lessons is for the teacher to ask a question and then call on a student to respond. While this provides an opportunity for one student to demonstrate understanding, the remaining students don't do so.

Another option would be for the teacher to allow all students to pair-share, respond with thumbs up or down, write their answers on small whiteboards and share their responses, or respond on handheld computers that tally the responses. Such activities hold each student accountable for demonstrating his or her understanding.

Beliefs That Support Rigor

As we think about the myths and what rigor is, we can describe our beliefs that support rigorous instruction. Each of these is crucial to how we teach in a rigorous manner.

> **Beliefs That Support Rigorous Instruction**
> - Rigor is not a negative concept. It is about meeting students where they are in their learning process and helping them move to a higher level of learning.
> - Every student should be given the opportunity to learn at high levels.
> - Students are more likely to succeed if they are held to high expectations and provided appropriate encouragement and support.
> - Rigor may "look" different for different students, but all students master complex, higher-order skills and concepts.
> - Students need varying levels of support as they move to more rigorous work.
> - A classroom environment that promotes student motivation, student ownership and empowerment, and a growth mindset is critical.

Scaffolding: A Critical Component of Rigor

Support and scaffolding are critical for student success. However, I've found that scaffolding can be misunderstood. For example, when I was a student, if someone needed help, they were pulled out of class, put in a corner, and given extra worksheets to do. I have no idea if the level or the practice was appropriate. One of the lessons I learned was to never ask for extra help.

Much later, as a consultant, I was visiting a high-poverty school that was struggling with test scores. I was leading an evaluation team designed to provide feedback to the teachers. I visited a science classroom and noticed that some students were working on an informational sheet about plants. When a student asked for help, they were given an alternate sheet that simply required them to color the plant. When the team met, we realized that was the major scaffolding strategy: coloring.

When a student is struggling to learn, he or she needs assistance. B. K. Garner, in *Getting to Got It*, points out that students use cognitive structures to process information and create meaning in four ways.

> Making connections
> Finding patterns
> Identifying rules
> Abstracting principles

Struggling learners have difficulty in one or more areas. Our role is to help them process information correctly and create meaning that is correct and that makes sense. Throughout this book, we'll be focusing on a variety of strategies that do so with an eye toward helping students learn at rigorous levels.

Beliefs About Scaffolding

Scaffolding may be needed by any student, depending on the learning situation.

Scaffolding may be provided for all students or with specific students, as needed.

Scaffolding is positive, not punishment.

Scaffolding leads students to rigorous learning.

Scaffolding supports independence.

Scaffolding May Be Needed by Any Student, Depending on the Learning Situation

First, I've found that scaffolding may be needed by any student. For example, when I was a professor at a university, I taught graduate students—teachers working on a master's degree. You might think they wouldn't need any extra help; after all, they have made it this far. However, I taught an advanced research paper that was unlike anything they had written before. Because of this, they needed scaffolding for the assignment. I broke it down into chunks, modelled the type of writing, and led writing conferences for feedback. One of my students said, "I didn't think I needed help, but I wouldn't have been successful without it."

It's easy to identify students who regularly struggle. It's less so when you have honors students who are struggling and hiding their needs. Part of effective instruction is identifying all students who need help.

Scaffolding May Be Provided for All Students or With Specific Students, as Needed

Second, scaffolding may be needed for your entire class, such as in the previous example with my graduate students or with certain students. The art of scaffolding is determining what scaffolding is needed but who needs it. If you are teaching a new or complex strategy, you may need to use some standard scaffolding skills with all students to ensure success. However, you will have times where a small number of students need additional scaffolding. Both are appropriate.

Scaffolding Is Positive, Not Punishment

Oftentimes, students are afraid of asking for help. They may be ashamed, or they may not want other students to laugh at them. It is part of our job as a teacher to help students understand that needing and accepting help is a normal part of the learning process. When we "make" them stay after school without offering other options, students view scaffolding as punishment. When we give students pages of extra practice, students view scaffolding as punishment. Let's create opportunities that students see as positive and supportive.

Scaffolding Leads Students to Rigorous Learning

Effective scaffolding always leads students to rigorous learning. When we make a decision to simply "dumb things down" so students can be successful, we are depriving them of the opportunity to learn at high levels. For example, simply giving students something easier to read may help them feel good, but using a process where student read an easier text then move back to something more complex once they have built background knowledge and vocabulary allows student to succeed at a more rigorous level.

Scaffolding Supports Independence

Finally, scaffolding supports independence. Sometimes, perhaps unintentionally, we provide support in a way that encourages students to become dependent on us. They can develop learned helplessness, a set of learned skills where students don't even try on their own—they simply look to us for answers. This is not what we want for our students. We want to provide scaffolding, lessen it over time, and encourage students to try on their own.

Coming Up

Throughout the remainder of this book, we'll be looking in-depth at the various areas of scaffolding. Each chapter is practical and geared for grades Pre-K-12. In Chapter 2, we'll explore the role of planning in scaffolding, including looking at several sample lesson plan excerpts. In Chapter 3, we'll focus on scaffolding in Classroom Discourse, and in Chapter 4, we'll discuss scaffolding for Vocabulary across the Content Areas. In Chapters 5 and 6, we'll examine Scaffolding in Comprehension across all Subject Areas and Writing across the Curriculum. Throughout all four of those chapters, you'll find a wide range of specific strategies. In Chapter 7, we'll investigate the role of formative assessment in scaffolding as well as sample strategies. The importance of specific emotional and social skills as scaffolding strategies is our topic in Chapter 8, and then we'll finish with common concerns such as parent partnerships.

I hope you will view the book as a scaffolding toolkit—one you can return to over and over again as you need a strategy. Think of reading the text as a journey; I hope you find some hidden treasure. You might find an idea or find something you can adapt, and if you do, I hope you'll contact me and let me know of your success. You can contact me through my website at www.barbarablackburnonline.com.

2
Planning for Scaffolding Instruction

Effective scaffolding simply doesn't happen without planning for it. I talked to one teacher who told me she was so experienced she didn't really need to plan her lessons. I politely disagreed. The best teachers I've met, regardless of their experience or expertise, agree that scaffolding on the fly doesn't meet all students' needs. In this chapter, we'll focus on planning strategies for scaffolding instruction.

> Acceleration vs. Remediation
> Planning Curriculum
> The Planning Process
> Incorporating Scaffolding in Your Lessons

Acceleration vs. Remediation

One important concept to discuss is the notion of acceleration vs. remediation. In the past, we often focused on a remediation approach with struggling students. After diagnosing a student's needs, we would teach at that level and move students forward from there, which usually occurred at a slow pace. I know that, when I was a Title One teacher, that was our approach, and, at the time, it was considered effective. However, if a student was working two grades below level, a year of remediation meant he or she had made progress but was still two grades below level. Students never caught up.

When I left teaching, I worked as a consultant for Scott Foresman Publishers. They published a reading series called *Focus*, which taught grade level skills to struggling students at their levels. It was considered innovative, but many teachers didn't believe it would work. The series used an acceleration approach—addressing lower-level needs but also teaching grade level content.

After COVID-19, we have so many students who are behind in learning, and they are struggling to catch up. What we are finding is that, if we don't focus on acceleration to move students forward, they will always be behind. As you plan, you'll want to make sure you are incorporating rigorous, accelerated learning into your instruction.

> **Acceleration Strategies**
> Analyze critical missing knowledge and skills.
> Build background knowledge and vocabulary.
> Prioritize content and standards.
> Personalize instruction.
> Monitor and adjust.

Let's take a quick look at each of these. In order to accelerate learning, you'll need to know what's missing in terms of knowledge and skills. The only way you can move on is to know what you need to address. Closely related to that is building background knowledge and vocabulary. In many cases, that is what's missing, so you'll want to focus on those areas.

Next, rather than trying to "cover everything," prioritize the content and standards that are most important, which we'll address next. When you do that, you can personalize instruction to what students need. Finally, continually monitor and adjust to ensure you are providing a laser-focus on acceleration.

Planning Curriculum

I want to take a moment to share a specific strategy related to prioritizing content and standards, one part of accelerating learning. Heidi Hayes Jacobs and Allison Zmuda, in their book *Curriculum: Using the Storyboard Approach to Frame Compelling Learning Journeys*, share a simple way to plan how to prioritize curriculum. They suggest you look at your curriculum and divide it into four areas.

I like this approach because they don't just say "cut stuff." They do recommend making decisions on cutting information, but they also suggest looking at simply cutting back some material, consolidating other ideas, and creating what you need to. This approach can help you truly accelerate learning for your students.

Planning for Prioritizing Curriculum			
What to Cut Out	What to Cut Back	What to Consolidate	What to Create

The Planning Process

There are a variety of ways to plan. When I was a first-year teacher, I simply looked through my resources, planned my lesson, and matched it to an objective. Then, I wrote or adapted a test or project to measure what my students learned. Now, I know that wasn't the best way. However, that process is still used in some classrooms for planning instruction and assessment. But this doesn't necessarily ensure rigor.

An alternative I prefer is the Task Cycle. I researched this model from the DuPont Corporation while working on my doctorate. The Task Cycle focuses on starting with the rationale (or purpose) and desired result (product) before determining the process or resources needed.

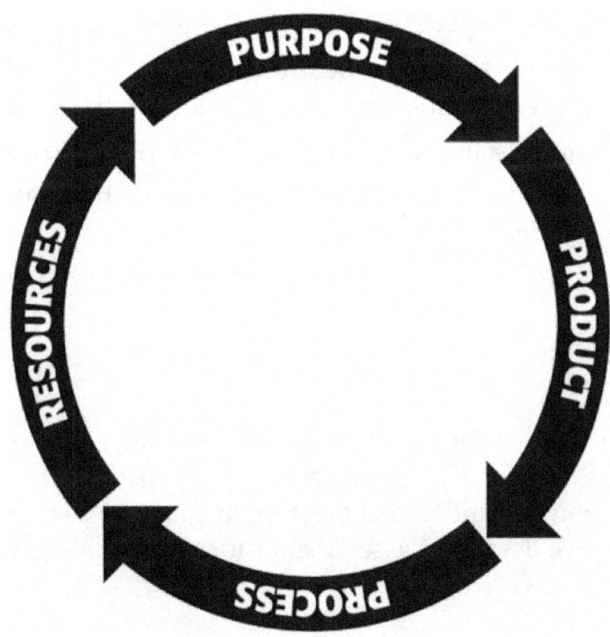

Think about how this applies to the classroom. Too often, we start with the process (how to get there) and resources (what we use to teach). For example, perhaps what I plan is for students to learn about Martin Luther King, Jr. and the Civil Rights Movement by viewing (process) his "I Have a Dream" speech online (resource).

Let's turn that around with the Task Cycle. The purpose is that we want students to understand the impact Martin Luther King, Jr. had on the Civil Rights movement (purpose) and we want them to demonstrate their understanding through a podcast (product). To do that, students will need to read about Martin Luther King, Jr. and watch the "I Have a Dream" speech (process) using online news articles and the video (resources).

By starting with our purpose and product, which is the assessment, we can ensure a higher-quality, more rigorous lesson. As we move forward in our discussion of the Task Cycle, we will be focusing specifically on process, especially the scaffolding that occurs.

Purpose

The first part of the Task Cycle is to decide on the purpose. The purpose will be embedded throughout all parts of the cycle. You'll typically consider your standards, goals, objectives, or learning targets to determine your purpose. No matter how you decide on your purpose, there are several questions to consider.

Questions

Did I match the essential knowledge and skills to the assessment?

Do students understand what to do and how it relates to the purpose?

Do I know how well the students understand the goal, standard, objectives, or learning targets?

Product

After you have determined your purpose, then you decide on the product or the assessment. Since there are a variety of assessments to choose from, you'll want to make sure you plan the best type to match your purpose. We'll address assessment more fully in Chapter 7, but let's do a quick overview.

> **General Principles**
> Match the type of assessment to the purpose.
> Incorporate rigor throughout the product.
> Stay on track.

First, match the type of assessment you want to use with the purpose of the assessment. For example, if you want students to demonstrate knowledge of facts, the best assessment may be a multiple-choice question or a short-answer question that requires a list response. But if you want students to demonstrate problem-solving skills as well as an understanding of cross-pollination, a performance-based assessment such as the design and completion of an experiment is appropriate.

Next, incorporate rigor throughout the assessment. As we explore the different types of assessment throughout the book, I'll include specific recommendations for rigor for each type. For now, generally, you should:

- include a focus on higher-order thinking skills;
- include problem-solving;
- include justifications and explanations in responses.

Finally, be sure you don't get off track. Recently, I was assessing samples of student assignments in elementary, middle, and high schools. One consistent theme I discovered was that many assessments were very creative, but the academic work was not rigorous, nor did they match the goals, standards, objectives, or learning targets. I am a huge believer in creative, engaging activities, but if the assessment is focused on that, you can miss the academic piece. For the samples I evaluated, students spent the majority of their time on the artistic, creative side of the assignment, whether it was creating a flipbook or a Prezi. The assessments provided evidence of students' creativity but less about their understanding of content. It's particularly important to balance the two.

Process

In the process part of the cycle, you work backwards from your product. Now that you know where you want to end up, you figure out how to get there. Planning how you teach a lesson is where your creativity can thrive, and it's where your scaffolding is critical. As you plan each activity, ask yourself, "If someone needs extra help, what should I do?"

Lesson Activity	*Scaffolding Support*

Scaffolding is the focus of our book. As we move into the following instructional chapters, we'll look at specific scaffolding strategies for the areas of Classroom Discourse, Vocabulary, Comprehension, and Writing. This will allow you to have a toolkit of approaches for your instructional planning. For now, here's a sampling of effective scaffolding strategies.

> **Sample Scaffolding Activities**
> Anchor Chart
> Graphic Organizer
> Coding and Highlighting
> Chunking
> Visualizing
> Thinking Guide
> Guide-o-Rama
> Modeling
> Layering Meaning

Resources

The final part of the Task Cycle to consider is the resources needed, especially for those who struggle. Do you need audio books or leveled texts? Do you need highlighters or reading guides? Consider what you need as you plan

Incorporating Scaffolding Into Your Lesson

Another critical scaffolding tool is the use of differentiated instruction. As you provide different ways of learning the content for different groups of students—whether they are grouped by readiness or interest—they are more likely to be successful. Whether you use a formal, differentiated approach or not, you'll want to provide adjustments for struggling students. Let's look at three lesson excerpts, starting with an elementary reading lesson.

Elementary School Reading Excerpt: Reading a Story	
Teacher previews a picture book for all students, pointing out key elements and any new vocabulary. Then, he or she reads the book aloud, stopping to ask questions as appropriate. You will need copies for all students.	
Scaffolding for Struggling Students	**Standard**
Teacher meets with students in small group. Teacher re-reads the book aloud, stopping to ask additional focused questions to ensure comprehension. Together, the group writes a short summary of the book.	Students work as book buddies to re-read the book. They can read silently, use choral reading, or take turns. Next, they work together using a reading guide to answer questions and summarize the book.

Typically, other application activities would follow, including writing activities.

Next, let's look at a more detailed lesson for the math classroom. Although this is a lesson with fractions, the scaffolding strategies are appropriate for all levels.

Fractions Differentiated Lesson

The teacher starts with activating prior knowledge and a review of proper fractions, such as 2/3, then continues with a discussion of mixed numbers (1 1/3) with examples of each type of fraction. Next, students briefly practice identifying the two types by circling "mixed," given a list of fractions. Some students work alone, others work with a partner, and the teacher may pull a small group for extra instruction. After they have completed this activity, students generate a T-chart of proper fractions and mixed numbers. Some students are given a list of fractions to categorize on the chart; others generate their own. Although these are lower level activities, they are likely necessary for students to move forward. Minimal tiering was used in this part of the lesson.

The teacher then shifts to solving problems using both proper fractions and mixed numbers. He or she follows a process similar to the one described previously. Next, students are provided structured tiered tasks, building to rigorous tasks in the second activity.

Scaffolding for Struggling Students	Standard Students
Teacher works with small group to review whole class instruction, then students are guided through the process of generating their own mixed numbers and solving simple algorithms. With guidance, students solve one simple word problem that uses proper fractions and mixed numbers.	Students work in pairs to apply the information by creating new algorithms using proper fractions and mixed numbers. They switch problems with a second pair and solve the problems. Next, each pair chooses an algorithm and uses it to create a word problem.
With guidance, students are given two simple word problems that include proper fractions and mixed numbers. The problems include the solution. They identify which of the two word problems is not solved correctly and why. The small group is divided into two groups. With guidance from the teacher, each group creates their own set of two problems, one of which is not correct. They swap sets with the other group, who must follow the same process as described earlier.	Students are provided a set of three word problems that include proper fractions and mixed numbers that have been solved. They are told that one of the problems is incorrect. They are asked to identify which of the word problems is not solved correctly, solve the problem correctly, explain why the original problem was not correct, as well as describe their solution and explain why it is accurate. Next, students create their own set of two problems, one of which is not correct. They swap sets with another student, who must follow the same process as described earlier.

Third, let's view a content literacy example for science that can also be used across other content areas.

Content Literacy Differentiated Lesson	
Scaffolding for Struggling Students	*Standard Students*
Students are given an article on the same topics that is written at a lower reading level than the standard text. Using a detailed "Thinking Notes," they read the text, with the teacher's assistance, as needed. Next, they answer comprehension questions, which are provided in advance.	Students read the grade level article. A standard "Thinking Notes" is provided that students can choose to use. Next, they answer comprehension questions.
Students read the grade-level article. While reading the lower-level text, students have built vocabulary and background knowledge, ensuring they are more successful with the grade-level text. Using a detailed "Thinking Notes," they read the text, with the teacher's assistance, as needed. Next, they answer comprehension questions, which include opportunities to compare and contrast information.	Students read a second article, one that is written at a higher level. A standard "Thinking Notes" is provided if they need it. Next, they answer comprehension questions, which include opportunities to compare and contrast information.

Class Discussion	
Scaffolding for Struggling Students	*Standard Students*
Students choose one of the identified issues related to oceans. Appropriate resources are provided. With the teacher's guidance, they create a three-column chart with the heading of: issue, how changes have affected people, and how they would address the situation. Students write a narrative explaining how the issue is impacting oceans including justification for their points. They may also propose a solution for the issue, with details.	Students may work individually or in pairs. After choosing an issue related to oceans, students research the topic in more depth. They find at least two sources, one of which is an editorial, website or promotional materials for an advocacy group, or some other type of opinion about the issue. Next, they evaluate the credibility of their opinion piece, comparing it to the factual information found in other sources. Finally, they write a critique of the editorial, website or promotional materials, or other type of opinion. The critique should include their opinion as well as a justification of their points, which includes factual information. They conclude with their own opinion as to a solution as well as an explanation of it.

Analysis of Historical Documents	
Struggling Students	*Standard Students*
Students work in groups of two or three. After selecting an approved time period, they work together to discover a significant economic, political, or social challenge faced during the time. With teacher guidance and a provided list of online sources, students choose three documents or artifacts from the era.	Students may work individually or in pairs. Students choose a time period. Through research, they determine significant economic, political, and social challenges faced during this time. Selecting one to focus on, students locate five primary source documents from the era.
Next, students watch a video about primary source analysis to see how a historian goes about determining the authorship, biases, credibility, and relevance of the document/artifact. Following this modeled process, the teacher leads the small group in their first analysis and facilitates the second source's analysis. The students complete the third source analysis together without teacher guidance. Students are given a graphic organizer to help them make comparisons between the documents so that conclusions can be drawn more effectively. Using a digital tool that is most familiar with them, students prepare a presentation that justifies whether or not the sources presented accurately and adequately represent the particular challenge of the time period. If needed, a suggested template or sequence for the presentation is provided. Students can use their graphic organizer as their handout.	Next, students evaluate each source for authorship, biases, credibility, and relevance. Then, taking the collection of gathered documents and artifacts into account, they draw appropriate and meaningful conclusions based on said evidence. Finally, they prepare to justify whether or not the sources presented accurately and adequately represent the particular challenge of time period. The presentation must include students' choice of the digital visuals, verbal speech, and informative handout for peers.

These four lesson excerpts show you options for working with small groups of students who need extra help. However, you can also provide extra scaffolding within a large group if that is more appropriate. For example, you may give certain students a graphic organizer to use during reading, writing, or watching a video. Or, some students may read a lower-level text while others are reading one that is more challenging. Finally, there may be students who learn more effectively with a partner or in a small group. We'll be focusing on a variety of strategies in the remaining chapters.

Key Ideas

- Intentional planning to incorporate scaffolding to accelerate learning makes a difference for students.
- Prioritizing curriculum means thinking about what to cut out, what to cut back, what to consolidate, and what to create.
- Planning using a backwards design approach can help you increase the effectiveness of your lessons.
- Scaffolding in action means adding appropriate support at the right time.

Thoughts to Consider

1. What are two or three main points you learned?
2. What is one strategy you would like to implement?
3. What is a question you would like to explore in more depth?

3

Scaffolding Classroom Discourse

Classroom discourse, whether it is informal talk, small group conversations, or a whole group discussion, is an integral part of your classroom. In this chapter, we'll look at six aspects of discourse and scaffolding.

> Elements of Successful Discourse
> Creating Instruction to Help Students Succeed
> Designing Questions that Support Scaffolding
> Using Roles and Responsibilities to Scaffold Small Group Work
> Types of Whole Group Discourse Activities
> Other Activities for Discourse

Elements of Successful Discourse

Before we can discuss scaffolding practices, we need to take a moment to talk about what successful discourse is. Too often, we accept what is simply noise—students talking, perhaps off-topic, often over each other. That's not discourse. Discourse is "classroom talk." It is on-topic, it uses academic vocabulary, and students listen just as much as they talk. Let's look at the nine characteristics of effective DISCOURSE.

> *Disagreements are handled respectfully*
> *Indicators of success are well-defined*
> *Students participate equally and equitably*
> *Clear directions are given*

> *Open-ended opportunities are provided*
> *Use of wait time and scaffolding is appropriate*
> *Raise the level of talk with academic vocabulary*
> *Students ask questions in addition to answering them*
> *Everyone is successful*

Disagreements Are Handled Respectfully

First, it's essential to a culture of positive discourse that students are respectful of each other, especially when they disagree. Arguments, name-calling, or other negative comments should be quickly redirected or shut down if necessary.

> - **Validate:** *"What I found most interesting (or alarming or questionable) was . . ." "I appreciate how you . . ."*
> - **Summarize:** *"So what I think you're saying . . ." or "To summarize what this you are thinking . . ."*
> - **Question:** *"I have a question I'd like to ask . . ." "Could you tell me more about that, please?"*
> - **Connect:** *"Your thoughts remind me of . . ." or "This makes me think of . . ." "I understand . . . , but I wonder . . ."*
> - **Evaluate/Critique:** *"Have you ever considered . . ." "What if we looked at it from another viewpoint?" "Maybe we could consider . . . instead."*

Just as we want students to respect each other, they need to recognize another student's point of view. It doesn't mean they have to agree; they just need to acknowledge there can be different points of view. If you are discussing a controversial issue, you'll want to be careful that arguments don't ensue. I suggest using sentence prompts for students to focus the conversation.

> *I agree with you because . . .*
> *Can you clarify/explain more . . .*
> *Can you help me understand . . .*
> *I'm not sure if I agree because . . .*
> *I don't agree, but I see what you are saying about . . .*

Another alternative is to incorporate writing as a part of class discussions. When 9/11 occurred, I faced a situation I was not expecting. I wanted my students to have the opportunity to share their feelings and ask questions, so I provided a time for open discussion. The second student who spoke asked a question that reflected a very controversial viewpoint. I stammered a bit, trying to respect the student and correct the misconception, but the damage was done.

The remaining students were so shocked and offended by the question, they shut down, and the helpful conversation I imagined completely collapsed. That one unexpected student comment changed my classroom climate. I was never able to rebuild the trust between that student and her classmates, but I did take away a valuable and lasting lesson.

What I learned is that classroom discussions, while critical, often may not be the best way to respond to a sensitive topic or situation. As I explored other options, I discovered that, if I use writing instead of talking, I could honor all students' voices, give them an opportunity to process their feelings, and build a foundation for discussing events or content in a more structured manner. With writing, I provide students an opportunity for ownership while retaining some control over what is said.

One strategy I use is a mind dump. I ask students to write or draw everything that is in their head—how they feel, what they think, and what they know or don't know—on a sheet of paper. It's their chance to take everything that is overwhelming them and get it out. There's no limit—they can do part of a page or multiple pages.

Next, I use one of two methods. For more structure or with an event that is more controversial, I may take up the papers and share different points as I scan them, giving students an opportunity to expand on what I've shared. Or I might use small groups and give them an opportunity to have some small-audience dialogue, using their papers as starting points. This also has the advantage of allowing students time to reflect before they talk. Then, I can lead a class discussion.

Written conversation is a strategy that works very well with students who feel less comfortable sharing their ideas verbally. The teacher will pair students in groups of 2–4 and provide a prompt such as "discuss the motives of the protagonist in chapter 12" or "explain how this painting supports what you know about Washington crossing the Delaware." Oftentimes, a print or non-print text is used as an anchor, but it is not required. In a math class, the teacher could simply use a word problem and ask students to begin describing how they would approach the problem. Each student is given a different color pen or marker and a large sheet of shared poster. Once students' initial thoughts are recorded on the paper, they begin responding to one another's thoughts and ideas with questions or comments of their own. The conversation continues until the teacher calls time or the students arrive at a common ground in their thinking. All of the collaboration is done without speaking. It's simple for the teacher to see each student's contributions to the discussion since they each wrote in a different color.

Ideas for Using Written Conversations

English/Language Arts: Use a poem or selection from a novel and ask students to discuss how figurative language or word choice or syntax impacts the tone or mood. Have a large copy of the text for students to annotate and margin write as part of their conversation.

Science: Use an informative text or infographic to introduce a science concept and allow students to write about the concepts they're noticing and the questions they have. They will begin to answer one another's questions, which helps students construct their own learning together!

Social Studies/History: Provide a historical or cultural painting or song, and have students make connections to the time period/culture/historical figures you are studying in class.

Math: Have a series of math problems and ask students to solve each through written conversation and determine the commonality between them.

Tech Connection
Written conversations can happen digitally via a whiteboard tool such as Padlet, Canva Whiteboard, or Parlay.

Indicators of Success Are Well-Defined

Students need to understand "what good discourse looks like." In the next section, we'll talk about how to teach students to participate in good discourse. Here, let's just note how important it is to have a clear criterion for how they should talk, whether in large group or small group settings.

Lower Grades, Academic Conversations, Expectations			
	Beginning	*Moving Forward*	*Expert*
Remarks	I shared my thoughts.	I shared my thoughts with examples and reasoning.	I shared my thoughts with reasoning and asked my classmates for their feedback.
Responses	I listened to others' ideas.	I listened to others' ideas and responded with my thoughts.	I listened to others' ideas, clarified what I heard, and connected by responding with my thoughts.
Reflection	I thought about what I heard my classmates say.	I considered what my classmates had to say and looked for connections to my ideas.	With an open mind, I internalized what my classmates were saying and used it to grow my understanding.

Middle/High School Academic Conversations, Expectations			
	Below Expectations	*Emerging Conversationalist*	*Conversation Expert*
Contribution	The student added very little perspective or ideas to the discussion.	The student contributed to the discussion with general ideas.	The student contributed to the discussion with unique ideas that were grounded in evidence and reasoning while also pushing peers to think deeply.

(continued)

(continued)

Middle/High School Academic Conversations, Expectations			
	Below Expectations	*Emerging Conversationalist*	*Conversation Expert*
Engagement	Student did not show evidence of active listening.	The student was visibly attentive to peers and listened to their ideas.	The student listened to peers with an open mind, noted significant ideas, validated others' thoughts, and considered their perspectives.
Preparedness	There is little evidence that the student prepared for the discussion beforehand.	The student came prepared with general thoughts and opinions to share.	The student thoroughly prepared with bullet point notes and questions to ask the group.

Students Participate Equally and Equitably

I'm sure you have led or observed a class discussion in which a few students dominated the conversation. Other students were distracted or indifferent. I've certainly had that happen in my classroom, and my struggling students simply didn't participate. Some didn't think they had anything to offer, some didn't know enough about the topic, and some were intimidated by those who did participate. I found that I needed to make an effort to ensure that all students—especially my struggling ones—had an equal chance to participate. That might mean they were given extra support. In the section later in the chapter on feedback, I'll give you a process for helping students who don't answer correctly. For now, here are six ideas for ensuring that all students participate.

> Don't use raised hands as your basis for calling on a student.
> Call on random students.
> Log who you call on so you can ensure everyone participates.
> Use pair-shares before whole group share outs to facilitate success.
> Use guiding questions if someone needs help.
> Give everyone a certain number of chips they can use to answer.

Clear Directions Are Given

Just as students need to understand the outcomes of good discourse, they need to have directions to reach those outcomes. For example, if you have asked them to participate in a positive way, provide directions so they know what to do.

> **Guidelines for Effective Peer Conversation**
> L- listen with interest (sit up and lean in)
> E- eye contact with the speaker
> T- take turns (don't interrupt)
> S- share the air time (equal opportunities to speak)
> TALK!

Open-ended Opportunities Are Provided

The best discourse is based on open-ended questions, whether from you or another student. It's easy to ask the "who, what, when, where" questions, but they should be followed up with "how do you know" or "why is that true." There are times it is appropriate to ask a basic question such as "what is the answer." You may want to ensure everyone knows the standard information, or that may be the best starting point for your struggling students. However, to ensure rigor, it's always important to then ask for an explanation, justification, or evidence.

Open-Ended Questions	
English/Language Arts	*Math*
How do you know? How could we improve this paragraph? What do you think about using this word in this sentence? Which line(s) from the text led you to that response? Have you considered how a different punctuation mark would change the tone of your sentence?	How do you know? How could you solve this problem? What strategies helped you solve this problem? How do you know the answer is correct? How can you prove the theorem? What would happen if you tried to solve this with a different approach?
Science	*Social Studies*
How do you know? What could you change? What strategies helped you solve this problem? What would you change in the experiment? Why? What led you to that hypothesis?	How do you know? How are these different? What is a real-life example of our topic? How does this historical event relate to our world today? Which community worker would help you the most?

Use of Wait Time and Scaffolding Is Appropriate

Incorporating wait time into your classroom culture will help all students participate in discussions and discourse. Although some students can jump in with an immediate response, others need to think before they answer. This is especially true of struggling students, who are usually not sure of their answers. As a teacher, I didn't fully understand wait time. Rather, I didn't use it very well. During my second year, my assistant principal noted in my observation that I needed to improve my wait time. I had a friend visit my class and time me so I could better understand what was happening. After her visit, I told her, "I am really proud. I waited at least 30 seconds for each response." She smiled and said, "10 seconds, regular as clockwork."

Wait time can seem long, but it's usually longer to us than the reality. I adjusted my teaching to use three wait time strategies. First, I use a timer, whether on my watch or phone, to be sure I am waiting an appropriate time. Next, rather than just having dead time in the classroom, I ask students to "think, draw, or write" during the wait time, which allows them to process the question in a variety of ways. Finally, a friend of mine who is a kindergarten teacher has her students put their heads on their desk to think to shut out all distractions.

You'll also want students to use wait time with each other, whether in a whole group or small group setting. In addition to encouraging them to wait, it's important to provide them specific strategies to use.

Ways for Students to Use Wait Time

Count to 20 in your head.

If you want to say something without waiting, write it down or draw it.

Remember it's ok to need to think before you say something.

Raise the Level of Talk With Academic Vocabulary

One key indicator of discourse vs. conversations is the use of academic vocabulary. We'll address this in-depth later in Chapter 4, but for now, it's important to know that students should use the vocabulary that is appropriate for their subject and topic. For example, I overheard some primary math students talking, and one said, "you know, you just put them together." Students were confused, and finally, the teacher stepped in. "Are you saying you should add the two numbers together?" The student nodded, and everyone understood the problem. Using appropriate vocabulary is important.

Ways to Encourage Use of Academic Vocabulary

Give points for vocabulary words.

Post key words in a visible area or use a word wall.

Help groups build customized word banks to use.

Allow students to "ask a friend" when they aren't sure what word to use.

Students Ask Questions in Addition to Answering Them

One challenge to participation is when students get stuck or don't know what to say, and therefore, they don't say anything. In this case, we want to encourage students to ask questions in addition to focusing on answering them, which we can do by providing question starters. The goal is for other students to ask the starter questions so that the group can continue its discussion. This is also ideal in small-group settings.

Starter Questions
To Prompt More Thinking
♦ You are on the right track. Tell us more.
♦ You are onto something. Keep going.
♦ The teacher said there is no right answer, so what would be your best answer?
To Fortify or Justify a Response
♦ What is your opinion about . . . ?
♦ Why is what you said important?
♦ Explain how you got that answer.
To See Others' Points of View
♦ How is your process different from mine?
♦ Do you see another way we could come up with a solution?

To Consider Consequences
♦ How can we apply this to real life?
♦ What did you learn in another lesson that we can connect this too?
♦ How else can we use this?

Source: Adapted from: http://ptgmedia.pearsoncmg.com/images/9780205627585/downloads/Echevarria_math_Ch1_TheAcademicLanguageofMathematics.pdf

Kathy Bumgardner, a reading specialist for the Gaston County Schools in North Carolina, introduced me to the Question Matrix (Weiderhold, 1995). This grid crosses basic questions (*who, what, when, where, why,* and *how*) with verbs (*is, did, can, would, will,* and *might*) to create a matrix that addresses all levels of questioning. If you divide the grid into four quadrants, you'll notice the upper left addresses basic questions; the closer you get to the bottom right, the higher the level of questioning. Copy the grid on bright colors of card stock, cut the squares apart, and put a complete set in a plastic bag. You can use this in two different ways. First, students can use the starters to ask questions during a whole group discussion. Or, after students have read a portion of text or when you are reviewing for a test, put them into small groups and give each group a bag of cards. Each student draws a card and has to finish the question. For example, if I draw the question frame "How would . . .?" I might ask, "How would you react if you lived in a country that faced a famine?" Then, the rest of the group must answer the question. I have done this activity with hundreds of teachers in my workshops, and you can use these questions with almost any topic. It's interactive and engaging, but most importantly, it scaffolds learning for students.

Question Matrix						
What Is	When Is	Where Is	Which Is	Who Is	Why Is	How Is
What Did	When Did	Where Did	Which Did	Who Did	Why Did	How Did
What Can	When Can	Where Can	Which Can	Who Can	Why Can	How Can
What Would	When Would	Where Would	Which Would	Who Would	Why Would	How Would
What Will	When Will	Where Will	Which Will	Who Will	Why Will	How Will
What Might	When Might	Where Might	Which Might	Who Might	Why Might	How Might

Source: Wiederhold (1995)

Everyone Is Successful

Finally, in an environment that supports discourse, everyone is successful, no matter what their learning readiness is. If you'll intentionally use the strategies we've discussed, with an eye toward student success, you'll find you have raised the level of discourse in your classroom because students who feel successful are more willing to participate.

Creating Instruction to Help Students Succeed

Did you know there are two types of prior knowledge? There is content prior knowledge, which is what we typically consider. That's when we activate what students know about the content or topic. However, there's a second type of prior knowledge—strategic prior knowledge. That is the knowledge about the strategy students must use to learn; in this case, discourse. It's just as important for us to either activate their prior knowledge about discourse or provide them a base of knowledge to work from. How do we do this? We intentionally teach discourse.

Gradual Release

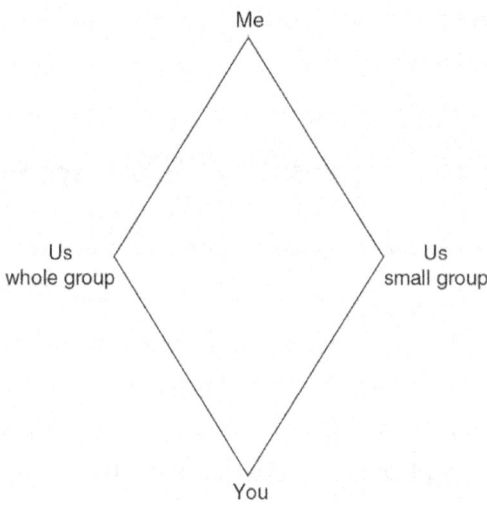

One way to think about teaching with an eye on scaffolding is with a diamond or rhombus. As you can see from the above figure, it starts with me (meaning the teacher). You begin by modeling a lesson. This might happen during a live lesson, or you might record something students may refer to regularly. Next, we go to us. There are two parts of this. First is the teacher and the students (us) following guided practice.

The second part of guided practice is "us," meaning students working with partners or in small groups. Finally, the student (you) does the work independently, which can happen in a variety of formats.

How do you decide when to move a student through the various stages of gradual release? I wish I could give you a set formula, but there isn't one. Sometimes students need to see you model something once; other students may need multiple explanations and models.

Jessica Neuberger uses modeling to prepare social studies students for their first student-led portfolio assessment conferences. As she explains:

> I recorded a sample interview to give the students a good idea of what to expect. When the class viewed the sample interview, I would stop the video after each question, have the students repeat each question to me and then they would write it down. The second time through, we watched the

whole interview with no interruptions. Then we discussed it. When I interviewed the students throughout the next week, they were prepared to share their work with me, offer me their opinions of their strengths and weaknesses, and we were able to set a goal for the next part of the year.

Because she knew this would be challenging for her students, she modeled the entire process for them and then provided scaffolded instruction to ensure their success.

Designing Questions That Support Scaffolding

A key part of instruction is designing the questions that are not only rigorous, but they scaffold student learning. Let's look at six strategies to DESIGN effective questions.

> **D**raft quality questions
> **E**ncourage multiple answers or more questions
> **S**caffold using supportive questions
> **I**nclude hints without giving away the answer, incorporate
> **G**ive students the opportunity to help each other
> **N**ote what "good" looks like.

Draft Quality Questions

In *Better Questioning for Better Learning*, Benjamin Johnson shares a strategy for creating quality questions that can help students learn. WILD HOG questions are designed for students to be successful, so the scaffolding is built in.

> **W**ritten
> **I**ntentionally *for*
> **L**earning
> **D**epth *and*
> **H**igher
> **O**rder
> **G**enius

In the rubric below, notice that questions are clear and direct. However, in the A-level questions, students are also working at a rigorous level.

WILD HOG Rubric			
Topic: Sovereignty and Suzerainty			
The students will effectively answer these questions:		Possible Grade	
	A Level	B Level	C Level
Content Knowledge	How can you show what sovereignty is and what suzerainty is?	How can you explain sovereignty and suzerainty?	What does sovereignty mean? What does suzerainty mean?
Content Understanding	What are the characteristics and actual effects of sovereignty and suzerainty?	What are the characteristics and intended effects of sovereignty and suzerainty?	What are the characteristics of sovereignty and suzerainty?
Application of Concepts	What are some examples and non-examples of sovereignty and suzerainty, and how do they compare with the historical examples found in the world?	What are some examples and non-examples of sovereignty and suzerainty?	What examples of sovereignty and suzerainty exist today?

(continued)

(continued)

WILD HOG Rubric			
Topic: Sovereignty and Suzerainty			
Analysis of Concepts	What are the pros and cons of sovereignty and suzerainty?	What are the similarities and differences of sovereignty and suzerainty?	What is the difference between sovereignty and suzerainty?
Evaluation of Concepts	What is the balance between the US and the 50 states in maintaining individual sovereignty and limiting suzerainty?	Which is more effective—sovereignty or suzerainty—for individual well-being? For the government?	Why do some prefer sovereignty over suzerainty?
Synthesis of Concepts	What international groups threaten the US sovereignty today and what should we do about it?	Is Puerto Rico sovereign, suzerain, or both? What would you suggest to them as a course of action in the future?	What did the founders of the Constitution have to say about sovereignty and suzerainty?

From Better Questioning for Better Learning: Strategies for Engaged Thinking by Benjamin Stewart Johnson.

Encourage Multiple Answers

When I was reading *Strategies for Developing Higher-Order Thinking Skills* by Wendy Conklin, I was excited to discover a model of questioning that I had not seen before, which encourages multiple answers. The Williams Model, developed by Frank Williams, has several aspects, but I want to focus on Wendy's types of questions that support the Williams Model.

> **Questioning Types**
>
> *Questions promote . . .*
>
> Fluency (generate many ideas)
>
> Flexibility (seek various objects or concepts, create various categories)
>
> Elaboration (expand or enrich content based on prior ideas)
>
> Originality (seek new ideas)
>
> Curiosity (question and wonder)
>
> Risk-taking (deal with new and/or unknown)
>
> Complexity (build structure in something that is unstructured)
>
> Imagination (visualize possibilities, move beyond the practical)

How does this work in practice? Let's look at a lesson for middle/high school art students, in which they are asked to critique a piece of art. You could also adapt it to other subjects, such as critiquing a musical performance or evaluating a science project.

Applying the Williams Model

\multicolumn{2}{c}{*Questioning in Practice: Critiquing a Piece of Art*}
Type of Question	*Prompts*
Fluency	Who would like this piece of art? What aspect would they specifically like?
Flexibility	Choose one element of the work of art. How does that change the overall piece? How might someone view it differently?
Elaboration	Take each key element of the artwork such as shading or color. Describe them in detail, including how they impact the overall piece.

(continued)

(continued)

Questioning in Practice: Critiquing a Piece of Art	
Type of Question	*Prompts*
Originality	If you were to use this piece of art to promote a cause or issue, what would it be? Why?
Curiosity	If the painting could speak, what would it say to the artist? To you?
Risk-Taking	Choose another type of art. It might be from a different time period, such as the Renaissance, or it might be a different format, such as a sculpture. Use it to change the work.
Complexity	What if the overarching theme of the artwork? What other elements support it? How do they do that?
Imagination	Imagine you are creating your own work. You'd like to include the best of what you see but improve upon it. What would you do?

Scaffold Using Supportive Questions

One way to scaffold questions is by using other questions that lead to the answer. For example, simply asking "Why would a democracy benefit people more than other governments" is quite challenging. You can build to that by asking questions such as "What are the benefits of a democracy?" and "How is that good for people?" You can do a similar set of questions for other governments, chart them on a poster or smartboard, and then ask students to use that information to answer the big question.

The following is an example of how supporting questions can be used to guide students in determining a theme for the novel *The Breadwinner* by Deborah Ellis.

> Essential question: How did the author reveal the theme through symbolism?
>
> *Scaffolding questions:*
>
> Teacher: Did you notice an object that recurred throughout the novel?
>
> Student: Yes. The author mentioned light and sunshine a lot.
>
> Teacher: Great! Let's think about what was happening when light was mentioned. What were the circumstances? How did the light impact the characters?
>
> Student 1: After Father was arrested, Parvana wanted to leave the light on so he could find his way home.
>
> Student 2: Nooria and Maryam sat the shaft of sunlight coming through the window on days when they felt trapped.
>
> Student 3: Nooria commented that she'd forgotten how a small thing like the sunshine could make her feel less depressed.
>
> Student 1: And at the end of the book, Parvana mentions that, through the dusty windshield, she notices the sun sparkling on the distant mountain top as they drive off to find Mother. This gives her hope that Mother is still alive.
>
> Teacher: Yes! So, in all of these instances, what was the light doing for the characters?
>
> Students: Providing hope when they felt like their situation was hopeless.
>
> Teacher: Great! And what lesson do you think Parvana and Nooria were learning when they realized how the light changed their perspective?
>
> Student 2: Maybe that even when your situation seems like a lost cause, you can find hope if you change the way you think about things.
>
> Teacher: That sounds like a thematic statement to me!

When I taught, one of my challenges was providing feedback during questioning. During a group discussion, if a student answered correctly, I knew to say, "That's exactly on point." Or "That's a great response that hits the nail on the head." But when a student was incorrect or only partially answered the question, I was stuck. What do you say then? How do you scaffold students to arrive at the solution rather than giving up on them? I created a feedback chart that describes how to handle each of those situations. It's also a great handout to leave for a substitute teacher, so they will know what to do.

Teacher Feedback Chart

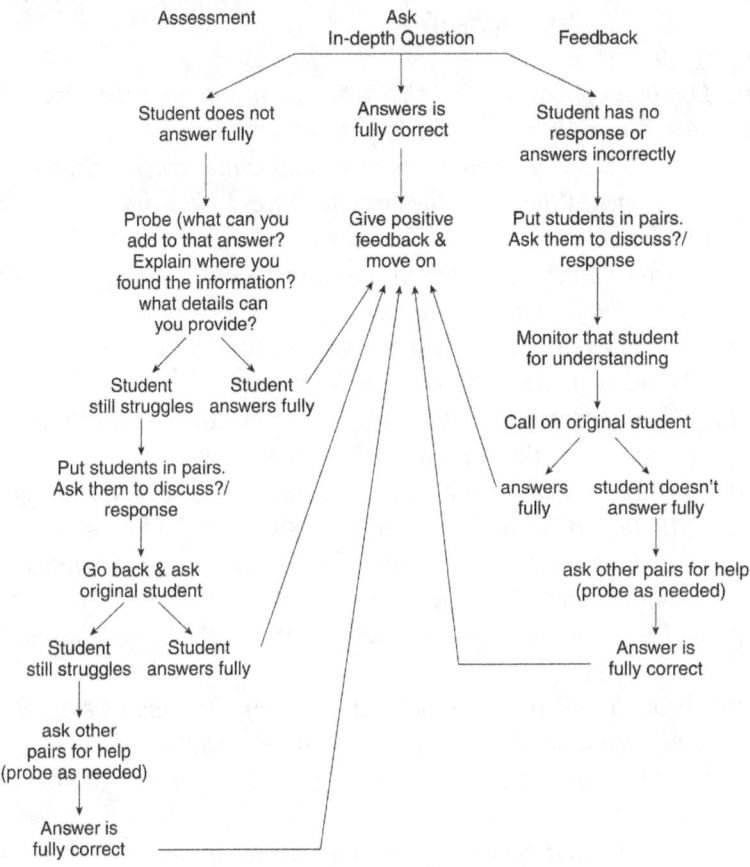

Incorporate Hints and Context in Your Questions

Just as you can use questions to scaffold learning, you can use hints and context. For example, instead of just saying, "What did Jacques Cousteau contribute to our society?", ask "By co-inventing scuba tanks, what did Jacques Cousteau contribute to our society?"

> ### *Sample for Younger Students*
> When you plant a seed in a cup, add water, and put it in the window, why does it grow?
>
> Knowing that chlorophyll allows plants to absorb energy from light, why do some plants lose their green pigment in winter?
>
> Because the Himalayan mountain range sits on the Indian and Eurasian tectonic plates, how does that impact the topography and changing height of Mt. Everest?

Similar to the Cousteau question, it's important to provide context. Prior to asking questions, review the main content, perhaps on an anchor chart. I also like to use a strategy called "Read the Room." Read the Room allows students to review materials from other students' perspectives. For any small group summaries, charts, diagrams, etc., that students complete, post them around the room. At the end of the lesson or at the beginning of the next day, students rotate through the posted material, "reading the room." This can spur discussion and support those students who are struggling.

Give Students the Opportunity to Help Each Other

It's important to allow students to help each other when needed. Ideally, students can respond on their own, but everyone needs help at times. I visited one classroom where the teacher mimicked *Who Wants to Be a Millionaire* and allowed students three lifelines to ask for help (poll the class, ask a friend, narrow down the choices). In another classroom, a high school history teacher allowed students to *contact the brain*, which meant they could ask their small group for help. Whatever you want to use is fine; just be sure students know it is acceptable to ask for help.

Note What "Good" Looks Like

Finally, be sure your question provides a clear indicator of success. For example, although both samples below are acceptable, notice how much more specific the second example is in each row.

Which story do you like better, and why?	Explain your choice using specific examples from the text and how it links to your life (be specific).
How did you solve the problem?	Justify your answer using what you have learned in class and using math words.

When you are writing questions, think about what you want. If you want an opinion, say so. If you want a student to provide evidence for their opinion, ask for that. Be clear about what you are looking for so that students can be successful.

Using Roles and Responsibilities to Scaffold Small Group Work

My at-risk students struggled with small group work, even after I taught everyone the basic principles of working together. I had some students who just shut down and didn't participate. Sometimes, it was simply too overwhelming for them, and other times, they didn't understand their place in the group. Both of these are addressed when you use assigned roles for group members. They do need to understand the whole picture, but they are able to focus on their part. It's critical that you not only provide specific roles, but you need to define them. For example, it's not enough to say, "You are the materials manager." Have a written job description.

Materials Manager
Collects materials for group.
Distributes material within group.
Replenishes supplies for the group.
Returns the materials to the supply bin.

Sample Roles Within Math and Science Groups

- Project Manager—oversees the creation of subtasks and the delegation of each required task while ensuring that individual members are working toward the big picture.
- Strategy Analyst—continuously monitors and reflect on the approach to completing a task, including the effectiveness of the strategies used by the group.
- Reflector—analyzes the work the group is doing, continuously reflecting on the efficiency of the group and its progress in meeting the task goals
- Recording Secretary—ensures there's a written record of strategies, procedures, and data.
- Materials Manager—collects materials that are needed and returns them to their proper location after use.
- Researcher—designs a plan for how to obtain information and delegates search terms/tools to each member.
- Data Collector—records and organizes the data points for the group.
- Progress Monitor—checks scoring guide, directions, rubric to ensure the group is progressing toward the goals in an efficient manner.

Sample Roles Within Math and Science Groups
♦ Friendly Critic—looks for the mistakes, misconceptions, or calculation errors the group might be making and respectfully challenges the group to resolve inconsistencies together.

Sample Roles Within English Language Arts Groups
♦ Discussion Leader—develops X questions (with answers and page references) at different levels. Leads discussion. ♦ Artist—draws a picture that relates to the text and explains its significance. ♦ Diction Detective—evaluates the diction used by identifying figurative language, imagery, and/or thematic statements and discusses the impact of the author's choice of words. ♦ Craftsman—makes connections between the conflicts and characters and analyzes how they work together to drive the plot forward.

Sample Roles Within Social Studies Groups
♦ Historical Preservationist—connects the text to a primary source document or other image that will deepen your understanding of the content. ♦ Terminology Teacher—notes the academic terminology used in the text. Determines how to put it into a graphic organizer and provides examples/nonexamples to broaden your peers' understanding of the concepts. ♦ Connector—makes connections between the text we have read today and what we have discussed in class. Makes connections to how this relates to our previous unit in history and how it impacts the world we live in today.

Once you have assigned roles and ensured they understand what to do, be sure to let them know how they will be assessed, whether by their peers, you, themselves, or all of these. Ensure that part of the grade is based on their individual participation and part of the grade is based on group work. Providing a sample assessment is helpful.

This holistic rubric could be used to help students see and achieve the expectations for cooperative learning.

Cooperative Learning Rubric (Simple)				
	You're a Team Player 3	You're Working on It... 2	You're the Lone Ranger 1	Total for Each Category
G Group Dedication	I listened respectfully to my teammates' ideas and offered suggestions that helped my group.	I did listen to ideas, but I didn't give suggestions.	I was distracted and more interested in the other groups than my group.	Group Dedication I circled number 3 2 1
R Responsibility	I eagerly accepted responsibility with my group and tried to do my part to help everyone in my group.	I accepted responsibility within my group without arguing.	I quarreled and did not accept roles given by my group.	Responsibility I circled number 3 2 1
O Open Communication	I listened to others' ideas and tried to solve conflicts peacefully.	I listened to others' ideas, but did not try to solve conflicts.	I was controlling and argumentative to my group.	Open Communication I circled number 3 2 1
U Use of Work Time	I was involved and engaged; I encouraged my group the entire time we were working.	I tried my best the entire time we were working.	I was not involved and did not offer any suggestions for the good of the group.	Use of Work Time I circled number 3 2 1
P Participation	I was a team member. I offered ideas, suggestions, and help for my group.	I participated in the project, but did not offer to help anyone.	I did not participate because I was not interested.	Participation I circled number 3 2 1
				Total_____

Copyright material from Barbara R. Blackburn (2025), *Scaffolding for Success: Helping Learners Meet Rigorous Expectations Across the Curriculum*, Routledge

Cooperative Learning Rubric (Complex)			
	You're a Team Player!	You're Working on It...	You're Flying Solo
G Group dedication	The student is totally dedicated to his or her group, offering all of his or her attention by actively listening to peers and responding with ideas.	The student is partially dedicated to his or her group though sometimes becomes distracted by students or issues outside the group.	The student spends most of his or her time focusing on things outside the group; he or she is not available for discussion or group work.
R Responsibility	The student shares responsibility equally with other group members and accepts his or her role in the group.	The student takes on responsibility but does not completely fulfill his or her obligations.	The student either tries to take over the group and does not share responsibilities or takes no part at all in the group work assigned.
O Open communication	The student gives polite and constructive criticism to group members when necessary, welcomes feedback from peers, resolves conflict peacefully, and asks questions when a group goal is unclear.	The student gives criticism, though often in a blunt manner, reluctantly accepts criticism from peers, and may not resolve conflict peacefully all of the time.	The student is quick to point out the faults of other group members yet is unwilling to take any criticism in return; often, the students argues with peers rather than calmly coming to a consensus.
U Utilization of work time	The student is always on task, working with group members to achieve goals, objectives, and deadlines.	The student is on task most of the time but occasionally takes time off from working with the group.	The student does not pay attention to the task at hand and frustrates other group members because of his or her inability to complete work in a timely fashion.
P Participation	The student is observed sharing ideas, reporting research findings to the group, taking notes from other members, and offering assistance to his or her peers as needed.	The student sometimes shares ideas or reports findings openly but rarely takes notes from other group members.	This student does not openly share ideas or findings with the group, nor does he or she take notes on peers'

Copyright material from Barbara R. Blackburn (2025), *Scaffolding for Success: Helping Learners Meet Rigorous Expectations Across the Curriculum*, Routledge

A more specific scoring guide may be used for older students. This allows for a pre-defined percentage of the grade to be based on group participation, while the bulk of the grade depends on individual contribution.

Your grade will be based on:
_____/10 Your individual notes in notebook
_____/10 Peer evaluation (anonymous)
_____/10 Your involvement in the verbal presentation
_____/40 Your Role:
   Visualizer: relevant infographic and image are included
   Project Manager: project plan and assignments are thorough with checkpoints and a completed rubric for the group
   Terminology Teacher: included five important terms with word map
   Connector: connections to historical event are strong and clear
_____/10 All sources are cited by the group
_____/10 Met cooperative learning expectations
_____/10 Spelling/Capitalization/Pronunciation of terms/Locations in presentation

---

Types of Whole-Group Discourse Activities

Although you may be accustomed to leading a whole group discussion, there are a variety of adaptations to that model. Let's look at:

Fishbowl
Morning Meetings
Paidea/Socratic Seminar
The Winner's Circle

Fishbowl

We also need to create other opportunities for our students to listen to each other. After students read a book or story, LaShana Burris at Cotton Belt Elementary School uses the "Fishbowl" activity to prompt discussion and encourage active listening. Three to five students are designated as fish, and they sit in a small circle. She gives the small group members a piece of "food," which is a slip of paper with an in-depth question written on it. As a school of fish, they discuss the answer to that question while the rest of the students sit in a larger circle around them and listen to the discussion (thus, the fishbowl).

As she explains,

> The people who are in the larger circle act as observers only. They use clipboards and paper to document a chosen fish's responses, behavior, and body language. After about five minutes of discussion, the observers share their notes with the fish they observed. After the last observer shares with the fish, the fish become observers and five of the observers become fish. The teacher gives the fish a different piece of fish food, or question to discuss. It encourages all students to actively read for comprehension, it is a vehicle for shy students to begin to participate, and it builds community.

Morning Meetings That Spark Discussions

Jenny Johansson creates listening opportunities for her special education students through inquiry-based morning meetings. For the first 5–20 minutes of class, she focuses on independent inquiry. Students generate questions on a variety of subjects and read books and articles about their topics.

> Then we get together in a circle on the floor for CPR [Circle of Power and Respect] for the actual meeting. During the independent inquiry time, they could sign up to actively participate in the meeting. The routine of the meeting includes a greeting, poetry, book recommendation, and inquiry sharing. During the greeting, they hear their name said in a positive light by their peers each day. During inquiry sharing students get to share with us what they are currently becoming an expert on. Student interests are really developed during this time.

During the discussions, she enhances the student's listening through involvement and ownership. As she notes, "They are so motivated by their own voices being heard."

Paideia or Socratic Seminars

Another type of discussion is a Paideia, or Socratic seminars, which shift the role of the teacher to that of a facilitator and emphasizes each student's contribution to the discussion. As Marcia Alexander, a high school teacher explains,

Paideia seminar has been the most successful teaching tool that I have used because it gives students the opportunity to demonstrate their knowledge and concerns about an issue that they can relate to. For example, I may have students read an excerpt written by Sojourner Truth, an African American ex-female slave, abolitionist, and speaker of women rights. The discussion topic is discrimination and I create open-ended questions, such as "Does being illiterate make a person less intelligent?"

In her role as a facilitator, Marcia ensures that every student speaks at least once before she poses another open-ended question. The nature of the discussion requires that students actively listen to each other in order to respond appropriately.

When I was teaching, I learned about the Paideia Seminar. A critical part of the seminar discussions was the notion of Socratic Questioning. Although some questions were provided for guidance, I still struggled with asking questions at the highest levels. In 2016, Richard Paul and Linda Elder provided a list of six types of Socratic Questions to nine categories. They are useful as you help students develop metacognition, or the concept of thinking about their own thinking.

Questions for a Socratic Dialogue	
Types of Question	*Samples*
Questions of Clarification	What do you mean by_____? What is your main point? Could you give me an example?
Questions that Probe Purpose	What was your purpose when you said _____? How do the purposes of these two groups vary? Was this purpose justifiable?
Questions that Probe Assumptions	What are you assuming? All of your reasoning depends on the idea that _____. Why have you based your reasoning on xxx rather than _____? Why do you think the assumption holds here?

(continued)

(continued)

	Questions for a Socratic Dialogue
Types of Question	*Samples*
Questions that Probe Information, Reasoning, Evidence, and Causes	What are your reasons for saying that? What led you to that belief? How could we go about finding out whether that is true?
Questions about Viewpoints or Perspectives	You seem to be approaching this issue from xxx perspective. Why have you chosen this perspective rather than that perspective? Can/did anyone see this another way?
Questions that Probe Implications and Consequences	What are you implying by that? Would that necessarily happen or only probably happen? If this and this are the case, then what else must be true?
Questions about the Question	How could someone settle this question? Can we break this question down at all? Why is this question important?
Questions that Probe Concepts	Do these two ideas conflict? If so, how? How is this idea guiding our thinking as we try to reason through this issue? Is this idea causing us problems? Which main distinctions should we draw in reasoning through this problem?
Questions that Probe Inferences and Interpretations	What information are we basing this conclusion? Is there a more logical inference we might make in this situation? Given all the facts, what is the best possible conclusion?

The Winner's Circle

I've adapted an idea from Jeffrey Wilhelm, which blends small group and whole-group instruction to help students understand a character or issue on a deeper level. Students work together in groups to plan questions and answers about a topic. Then, in a whole group, one small group is in the "winner's circle." The teacher and other students use the student-generated questions and ask the students in the winner's circle to answer. The students work as a "brain" to answer together, and if needed, they can expand to the larger brain (another group) to respond.

Other Activities for Discourse

In addition to whole-group discussion, you may want to incorporate other types of activities.

Pair-Shares

You may already use pair-shares or think-pair shares as a part of your classroom. Typically, during instruction, you ask students to reflect on the content, turn to a partner, and share the answer to a question. Then, several students share their answers with the whole group.

There's an easy way to switch this to make it more effective and more rigorous. When students share with the whole group, they share their partner's answer, not their own. This encourages them to listen better, and it requires their partner to do a better job explaining their answer.

Finally, Debbie Newman, in *The Noisy Classroom*, suggests a variety of adaptations to groupings that are guaranteed to engage all students—even your struggling ones.

Balloon Debate	The premise is that a variety of people (historical figures, scientists or mathematicians, or characters in a story or novel) are on a hot air balloon that is starting to sink. Each student assumes the identity of one of the people. They make a short speech as to why they should be saved, and the class votes.

(continued)

(continued)

Boxing Match	Divide the class into the Blue Corner and the Red Corner. One from each comes forward to "box" or make a point. During the back-and-forth exchange, if one is struggling, you can ring the bell to go back to their corners, where they can get help from their team.
Rebuttal Tennis	In pairs, students debate an issue. Partner A makes a point with a supporting reason, then Partner B does the same. They go back and forth "hitting the debate ball."
I Couldn't Disagree More	Students respond to statements on the board. The only rule is that students must begin their answers with "I couldn't disagree more."
Where Do You Stand	This works best as a starting point for discussions. Label one side of the room as strongly agree and one side as strongly disagree. Then put a line from the two labels. Start with the point, and students line up based on how they feel about your point. Then, they can discuss with nearby classmates.
Chat Show	Imagine Oprah or another talk show host. You can be the host, or you can assign a student to be the host. Start with a debatable point, and work from there!
Dragon's Den	This is similar to Shark Tank. Students pitch their ideas to a group of investors, who can be teachers, leaders, former students, or members of the community.
Quiz and Switch	Another good starter activity, students move around the room asking and answering questions about the topic.

Tech Connection

It can be very engaging to use digital tools when asking students to engage. PearDeck, NearPod, and Lumio are excellent online educational platforms in which you can create activities (or use pre-existing lessons), push content out to student devices, gather feedback, formatively assess students' conceptual understanding in real time, and immediately correct misconceptions. Using technology can ensure that all students are actively participating and learning simultaneously.

Key Ideas

- Understanding effective discourse will help you be more effective.
- Intentionally teaching discourse skills is help your students succeed.
- It's important to design effective questions to support scaffolding.
- Assigning clear roles and responsibilities gives support to students.
- Providing a range of activities helps students learn.

Thoughts to Consider

1. What are two or three main points you learned?
2. What is one strategy you would like to implement?
3. What is a question you would like to explore in more depth?

4

Scaffolding Vocabulary Throughout the Curriculum

Vocabulary is a strong indicator of student success. Because of this, it's critical to scaffold vocabulary instruction. I've found there are three key steps for effective scaffolding in vocabulary, each of which incorporates scaffolding.

> Create a Culture that Celebrates Vocabulary
> Intentionally Teach Key Vocabulary
> Allow Multiple Opportunity to Explore and Apply Vocabulary

Create a Culture That Celebrates Vocabulary

What does it mean to create a culture that celebrates vocabulary? Let's start with a negative example. I taught a student, Marianne, who hated vocabulary. She had always struggled in school, and she blamed words. As she said, "Words are just things teachers use to make students feel dumb." Of course, that's not true, but it is how she—and many other students—felt. We want to create a classroom environment that, at a minimum, helps students see the value and purpose of vocabulary. Let's look at three strategies for building a strong vocabulary culture.

> Our Attitude
> Friendly Texts
> Word Walls

DOI: 10.4324/9781003506560-4

Our Attitude

A mentor of mine once said, "A truly great teacher is someone who inspires their students to learn, even when they think they don't want to (unknown author)." I believe that teachers can shape student learning as well as students' attitudes and perspectives. If you are enthusiastic about something, your students are more likely to be enthusiastic about the same thing. If you don't like a particular topic, neither will they. So, the first step toward scaffolding vocabulary instruction is for you to have a good attitude about learning and teaching vocabulary, no matter your subject area. You might be thinking, "I don't teach vocabulary. That happens in reading/Language Arts/English!" Do you teach math? Vocabulary is critical to understanding how to solve problems. Do you teach physical education? Your students have to understand words and concepts to apply their learning. I could go on and on with every school subject, but you get the idea. Vocabulary is key for you—no matter your content area. Your first choice is to embrace vocabulary in your subject area and show that to your students.

Ways to Show Enthusiasm About Vocabulary

Inject enthusiasm into your voice when discussing vocabulary.

Smile when answering questions or addressing issues with vocabulary.

Use encouraging phrases with your students:

    I know you can figure this out.

    You've learned new words before; I know you can do it now.

    This word does seem challenging. What can we do together to make it understandable?

    I've noticed you are really using your knowledge of words to understand our text.

Allow students to see you struggle with and overcome vocabulary challenges.

Never complain about vocabulary instruction in front of your students.

We can also encourage a positive attitude toward vocabulary with celebrations. You probably already celebrate successes in your classroom.

I'm suggesting being intentional about adding vocabulary to your repertoire. For example, you can praise students for learning a new word, for figuring out a word they don't know, or for identifying a connection between words. You might praise verbally, use stickers, or provide reward certificates.

Sample Certificates

Victory with Vocabulary

Spying a New Word (in another class or outside school)

Connecting Concepts

Detecting a Definition

Making Letters Work Together

Mathematical Word Genius

Scientific Scholar

Social Studies Word Detective

Friendly Texts

I also found that it was important to incorporate texts in my classroom that were "vocabulary friendly." What does that mean? I look for books that use a variety of vocabulary in ways that make students laugh, help them see the importance of words, and make it easy to learn in new ways. For example, my favorite children's book is *The Phantom Tollbooth*. It is often used in elementary school, but I also used it through grade 9 with success. In the book, Milo, a boy who is bored at school and bored at home and bored by everything, finds a mysterious tollbooth. It takes him into the Kingdom of Wisdom, where he visits Dictionopolis, the city of words, and Digitopolis, the city of numbers. In Expectations, which is where you must go before you get to where you are going, he meets the Whether Man, not the Weather Man, because it is more important to know whether or not there will be weather than what the weather will be. See why I like it? My classes played with words throughout the book, interpreting the text at different levels depending on their age and grade level. A friend of mine used *A Gebra Named Al* with similar success for her students.

Picture Books for Word Play
Dr. Seuss Books
Bumblebee, Grumblebee
Max's Castle
Digging for Words
The Word Collector
Miss Alaneus and the Vocabulary Disaster
Who I Am

Upper Elementary/Middle School Books
Dr. Seuss Books (especially *Oh The Places You'll Go!*)
More than Words
One Grain of Rice
The Phantom Tollbooth
The Number Devil
The Season of Styx Malone

Middle/High School Books
Words on Fire
The Poet X
Fish in a Tree
A Gebra Named Al
The Power of Words (Churchill)
The Little Book of Lost Words
The Chemy Called Al

A second type of friendly texts is friendly dictionaries. When I was teaching young students, having a primary dictionary was critical. The one we used was organized by themes, such as farm or ocean, and the words and pictures all related to the theme. There are a wide range available now, both in print and online, such as the Oxford Children's Dictionary or the

WILD dictionary for K-2 by Wordsmyth. I also like the Collins COBUILD Dictionary, which uses more student-friendly definitions.

If you teach something other than reading/language arts/English, much of your vocabulary is specialized, which likely has a unique meaning. Therefore, you need something different.

Tech Connection

Math	Science
Amathsdictionaryforkids.com Mathisfun.com (K-12) Mathwords.com Wolfram Math World	World of Science Enchanted Learning (includes specialized dictionaries such as astronomy and botany) Visionlearning Glossary
Social Studies	**Others**
Ancient History Encyclopedia Online Dictionary of the Social Sciences Geography Dictionary and Glossary (ISTE)	Netlingo (technology definitions) Sportsdefinitions.com Museum of Modern Art dictionary Naxos.com(music) Inc. Com Encyclopedia (business)

Word Walls

Another strategy is to use your walls to celebrate and teach words. Word walls have been in favor for years, but you really can use all aspects of your walls. For example, when I was teaching, I posted new spelling words on the ceiling. Finally, a student noticed, and they were intrigued that I not only posted the words but left them up in case they needed help. My purpose, in part, was to teach them to find information when they needed it instead of just memorizing words. Ironically, they studied harder knowing they had extra assistance available.

First, I recommend having a specific word wall for your current instruction. Whether you are teaching vowel sounds, fractions, particles, types of government, or elements of art, there are key words and concepts your students need to know. You can post all the words in advance and refer to them throughout your lessons or post them as you teach. Be sure to place your words in a prominent place in your classroom.

Other Tips for Word Walls

Be sure your lettering is large enough to be seen throughout the room.

Be careful with colors—yellow looks bright, but it doesn't work well for the words themselves.

Put your word wall where students can see it clearly—that may be lower for younger students or higher for older students.

Add pictures for English Learners.

Remove words once they are generally understood. Make room for new words.

Next, I want to address two other common questions: space and working with older students. First, you may not have enough usable space for a word wall. In that case, I'd switch to personal word walls for students. Using file folders, notebooks, or shared documents, students develop their own word walls based on your instruction and guidance. I like using post-it notes for the words so students can rearrange them and remove words as needed.

Sample Personal Word Wall	
Lesson Words	*Review Words*
Words I'm Working On	Other Words

What About Word Walls With Older Students?

I'm often asked by middle and high school teachers, especially those who do not teach reading/language arts/English, why they should use a word wall. They aren't being disrespectful, just curious. Let me answer the two questions I'm most often asked. First, why are word walls important? It's simple. Word walls help students learn, especially those who struggle. Seeing words organized for them and used in instruction builds a base of vocabulary knowledge for your struggling students. If you add visual cues, it helps them remember the words more often.

Next, how do I find time to work with word walls? I already have so much to do. Don't think about a word wall being something else to do. Rather, it's a tool to support your regular instruction. Just like you might use a video or image to help students understand your lesson, the word wall does the same. Integrate it; don't make it extra.

Finally, especially for upper grades and content areas, here is a variety of resources that can help you get started.

Tech Connection

Consider allowing students to create a digital word wall with images, video links, etc., via Padlet, Canva, ThingLink, or Miro to track their own vocabulary development and understanding of word connections within your content area.

Other Resources	
General	*Social Studies*
♦ Eight Tips for Creating Word Walls in Secondary: www.readingandwritinghaven.com/8-tips-for-creating-effective-word-walls-in-secondary ♦ How and Why to Use Word Walls with Older Students: https://buildingbooklove.com/how-and-why-to-use-word-walls-with/	♦ Word Walls in Social Studies: www.socialstudies.org/sites/default/files/view-article-2020-10/se-8405020313.pdf ♦ Using Word Walls Successfully in Social Studies: www.socialstudiessuccess.com/2016/12/using-word-walls-successfully-in-social-studies.html

(continued)

(continued)

Other Resources	
General	*Social Studies*
♦ Word Walls: Supporting Literacy in Secondary School Classrooms: www.readingrockets.org/sites/default/files/migrated/content/pdfs/World_Walls_-_A_Support_for_Literacy_in_Secondary_School_Classrooms.pdf ♦ Tips for Setting up Middle or High School Word Walls: www.brainyapples.com/2020/02/10/setting-up-a-word-wall-in-middle-high-school/	♦ Early American History Word Wall: https://mrandmrssocialstudies.com/early-american-history-word-wall-a-how-to-guide/
Math	*Science*
♦ Mathematics Vocabulary Word Wall Cards (free) all grades: www.doe.virginia.gov/teaching-learning-assessment/k-12-standards-instruction/mathematics/instructional-resources/mathematics-vocabulary-word-wall-cards ♦ High School Math Word Wall Ideas: www.scaffoldedmath.com/2015/09/high-school-math-word-wall-ideas.html ♦ Middle School Math Word Wall Ideas: www.scaffoldedmath.com/2017/10/middle-school-math-word-wall-ideas.html	♦ Science Word Walls: https://theteachersupstairs.com/science-word-walls-2-painless-ways-to-effectively-use-them/ ♦ The Evolution of my Middle School Science Word Wall: https://keslerscience.com/the-evolution-of-my-middle-school-science-word-wall ♦ Using Word Walls in Science: www.socialstudiessuccess.com/2016/12/using-word-walls-successfully-in-social-studies.html

(continued)

(continued)

Other	
♦ Word Walls in the Music Classroom: https://study.com/academy/popular/music-word-walls.html ♦ My Music Classroom Has a Word Wall, Now What? http://melodysoup.blogspot.com/2012/09/my-music-classroom-has-word-wall-now.html?showComment=1347924792531 ♦ Taxonomy of Music Graphic: https://turnerkarl.wordpress.com/2012/10/11/finished-music-infographic/ ♦ Physical Education Word Walls: www.capnpetespower-pe.com/single-post/how-to-use-word-walls-in-physical-education-tips-and-strategies ♦ PE Word Wall: www.thephysed-teacher.com/pe-word-wall.html	

Intentionally Teach Key Vocabulary

As I discussed in *Classroom Instruction from A to Z*, although we have always known the importance of teaching vocabulary, there has recently been a focus on academic vocabulary, especially vocabulary tiers.

Tiers of Vocabulary

Tiers of Vocabulary were introduced by Isabel Beck and Margaret McKeown in 1987. As they describe them, Tier One words are acquired through everyday speech. These words are common and are typically taught at early grades or learned through everyday use around them. Tier Two includes academic words that appear across all texts. They may change meaning due to use and they present a challenge if experienced in text initially. Vocabulary instruction for these words typically adds to students' understanding of the meaning. Tier Three vocabulary is domain or content area-specific. They are critical for building conceptual understanding in content, but they need to be explicit instruction. These words are best taught when they are needed in the context of the lesson.

Sample Tier-Three Vocabulary	
English/Language Arts	*Social Studies*
Textual evidence	Latitude/longitude
Diction	Goods/Services
Fact/Opinion	Culture
Fiction/Nonfiction	Artifact
Biography/Autobiography	Historical
Analyze	Globe
Visualize	Continent
Character	Justify
Conflict	Label
Plot	Issue
Setting	Locate
Narrative	Primary vs. Secondary
Synonym/Antonym	Latitude/longitude
Plot	Per capita
Hyperbole	Democracy
Diction	Gross domestic product
Connotation	Topography
Metaphor	Nationalism
Theme	Secession
Rhyme scheme	Legislature
Characterization	Industrialization
Internal conflict	Democracy
Logos/pathos/ethos	Justification
Bias	

Math	*Science*
Add	Acid
Balance	Atom

(continued)

(continued)

Cube	Base
Dividend	Convection
Divisor	Environment
Estimate	Gas
Equation	Humidity
Factor	Mass
Pattern	Predict
Volume	Thermometer
Adjacent angles	Aerobic
Binomial	Atomic number
Conic sections	Carnivore
Dilation	Carbon cycle
Intercept	Heterozygous
Quadrant	Isotopes
Reciprocal	Magnetic field
Substitute	Velocity
Translation	Solvent
Variance	Work

Tier Two Words provide an opportunity for thorough vocabulary development. These should be words that you focus on in depth, since they will have applications not only in the specified text, but across other texts and areas of the curriculum.

> **Tier-Two Vocabulary**
> Notice
> Focus
> Problem
> Analyze
> Predict
> Compare
> Contrast
> Question
> Revise
> Infer
> Average
> Solution
> Declare
> Unique
> Diverse
> Persuasive
> Inhabitants
> Hypothetical
> Similar
> Proximity

Janet Allen's Academic Vocabulary

In *Tools for Teaching Academic Vocabulary*, Janet Allen organizes academic vocabulary by context. She explains there are four types of words: general academic words, domain- or discipline-specific terms, topic-specific vocabulary, and passage-critical words.

> **Four Types of Academic Vocabulary**
> General Academic Vocabulary
> Domain- or Discipline-Specific Vocabulary
> Topic-Specific Vocabulary
> Passage-Critical Vocabulary

First, there is general academic vocabulary, which is not discipline-specific. Students frequently see these words, such as analyze, synthesize, contrast, and restate. It's important to provide detailed instruction with lots of practice, so that students are very familiar with them.

Next, she describes domain- or discipline-specific words, which are frequently used within a specific discipline, such as science or math. These words include terms such as foreshadowing, hypothesis, rational number, or aerobic exercise. Within the content area, these words should be reinforced regularly.

Third, there are topic-specific words. They are needed to understand a specific lesson or topic and are typically critical to an understanding of the concept. Direct instruction is usually necessary with these terms. Examples include Holocaust, biome, and impressionism.

Finally, passage-critical words are those that are necessary to understand a specific text. These words are crucial to comprehension of the passage. Particularly for specialized words, direct instruction is needed. Janet explains that, in the book *BATS: Biggest! Littlest!*, sample passage-critical words include echolocation, horning, roost, and wingspan.

Whichever structure you use, thinking about the different types of vocabulary will help you teach words in a more meaningful way, as opposed to having students simply memorize definitions of random word lists.

Now that we've looked at types of words, we can consider which ones to teach as well as how to teach them. As a teacher, I considered the tier level, but I also thought about words that were confusing, such as some and sum or cent and sent. You'll want to consider your instruction and your students' needs when determining what words to prioritizing.

When I was teaching, there were two broad categories of instruction: deductive and inductive. Both have advantages, and I find these to still be helpful when thinking about how to teach vocabulary.

Categories of Instruction:
Deductive
Inductive

Deductive

Deductive instruction is teacher-focused. The teacher introduces and teaches vocabulary in a direct manner. What you think of as a traditional lesson is deduction. You can also find more information on explicit instruction in Chapter 5.

Inductive Instruction

If deductive teaching is like a triangle, with the teacher at the top, inductive is an upside-down triangle with the students at the start. In inductive instruction, the students start the lesson through exploration and investigation. That is followed by the teacher facilitating learning through a discussion of the activities. The teacher's role is critical in both types.

> Teacher's Role:
> Deductive: Directive
> Inductive: Facilitative

You can use a variety of activities for investigation in an inductive lesson, including many of those we'll discuss in the next section. However, as a starting point, two of my favorite activities are Three Alike and Red Herring. In Three Alike, you give three examples, such as Raleigh, North Carolina, Sacramento, California, and Albany, New York. If this is an introduction, students may use their prior knowledge to determine if these are state capitals. It's an ideal way for students to "play" with vocabulary as well as moving beyond memorization. A pre-kindergarten teacher can use it to introduce the color of the day, pulling items out of a box, or a science teacher can use this strategy to introduce elements or subatomic particles. It's also ideal for students to create the three words or concepts.

To increase the rigor, former teacher Lindsay Yearta uses the "Red Herring" game with her students. She gives multiple examples that are linked, but students must identify the red herring—the one that does NOT belong. For example, I might ask you to choose the red herring among Florida, California, Virginia, and Arizona. In addition to choosing Arizona, they must also justify their choice based on the fact that Arizona doesn't have a coastline. Again, students may create the Red Herring, and based on their responses, you can see how much they know.

Allow Multiple Opportunity to Explore and Apply Opportunities

A final part of scaffolding vocabulary instruction is to allow students to explore and apply what they've learned.

> **Ways to Explore and Apply**
> Reading
> Word Sorts
> Writing
> Games

Explore and Apply Through Reading

Immersing students in text that uses vocabulary allows students to apply what they have learned in context, which is more likely to cement their understanding. The caution is to choose the right text. For example, if you choose a difficult text, students may not be able to apply their new learning. Or, if you choose a text that is too easy, they may not have the opportunity for application. In Chapter 5, I discuss the strategy of layering meaning and provide a detailed list of sources for varying text. What I'll say here is that you can use the variety of AI generated tools to paraphrase and simplify text to provide different versions of the text for your students.

In this sample, the first is an excerpt from *The Geolology and Ore Deposits of the Virgilina District of Virginia and North Carolina by Francis Baker Laney. Public Domain Use.* Accessed through the HathiTrust. The second is the same passage with modifications from rewordify.com; the third is a very simple version from paraphrasetool.com.

> *Original*
>
> The character of the soil depends upon the nature of the underlying rock. The tuffs and other volcanics produce a lean, shallow soil; the granite produces a strong, rather sandy soil; and the other igneous rocks break down into a rather sticky but fairly strong soil. Of all the truly igneous rocks, the diabase produces the leanest and least desirable soil. The volcano-sedimentary rocks—the greenstone and sericite schcists—as a rule form a lean and shallow soil. Rock outcroppings are not numerous except along stream course, but almost invariably, the partially decayed rock is very near the surface.

(continued)

(continued)

Simplified with Explanations
The character of the soil depends upon the nature of the hidden (under) rock. The tuffs and other volcano-relateds produce a lean, shallow soil; the (very hard rock) produces a strong, rather sandy soil; and the other (created in a volcano) rocks break down into a rather sticky but fairly strong soil. Of all the truly (created in a volcano) rocks, the diabase produces the leanestand least desirable soil. The (place on the Earth where red-hot liquid rocks, ash, and gas sometimes flow or explode out) (coming from material that sinks in liquid) rocks—the greenstone and sericite schcists—as a rule form a lean and shallow soil. Rock (rocks sticking up from the ground) are not many except along stream course, but almost always the partially (rotted/became ruined or worse) rock is very near the surface.

Simplest
The type of soil depends on the rocks that are underneath it. Some rocks from volcanoes make the soil thin and not very good for growing things. Other rocks that are very hard make the soil strong and sandy. Rocks that come from volcanoes break down into sticky but strong soil. The diabase rock from volcanoes makes the worst soil. Rocks like greenstone and sericite schists also make thin and not very good soil. Rocks that stick out of the ground are not very common, but the rocks that have started to break down are usually close to the surface.

Explore and Apply Through Word Sorts

Another way students can explore and extend vocabulary is through word sorts. This is exactly what it sounds like. You start by giving students a set of word cards and ask them to sort them. Then, in groups or in a whole group, students discuss the words and their uses.

Ways to Sort Words
Letters or Sounds
Prefixes or Affixes
Synonyms or Anonyms
Centered around a Topic
What I Know and What I Don't Know

A specific word sort is actually mixed with a graphic organizer. Students create a concept map, with which they sort words and graphically demonstrate how they are connected.

Word Bank: (Teacher provides a list of words here). Students will come up with three different ways to group the words (not all words need to be used each time)		
Category #1– Words that belong in this category: Connection/ Rationale–	Category #2– Words that belong in this category: Connection/ Rationale–	Category #3– Words that belong in this category: Connection/ Rationale–

Tech Connection
Consider allowing students to use an online visual dictionary such as Snappy Words. The name may sound elementary, but this dictionary "groups synonyms into synsets through lexical relations between terms." For example, when searching the word "surly," the following is displayed; each related word is defined as the cursor is moved over it.

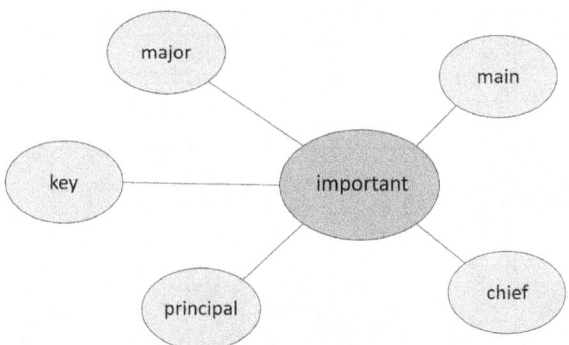

Explore and Apply Through Graphic Organizers

Graphic organizers are always a good tool to help students organize and extend their knowledge of vocabulary. As we just discussed, students can create word maps. But there are other, more formal graphic organizers that can help your students. Students can work on these maps individually or in small groups.

Using a graphic organizer, students discuss different elements of a particular vocabulary term.

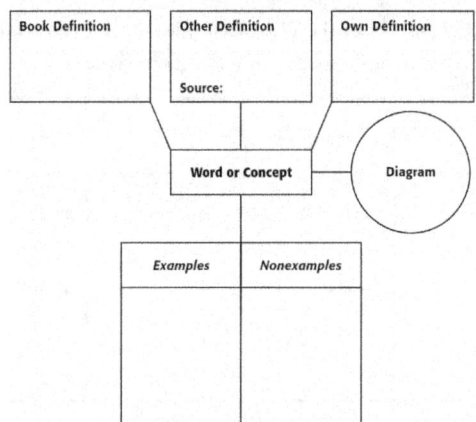

You can customize the headings on the organizer to match your specific subject area. The key to this process is that, as students explore multiple definitions, examples and nonexamples, and characteristics or functions, they develop a fuller grasp of the concept.

This simple table can be used when you want students to find ways a certain word or concept has been used under a variety of circumstances.

Where Have I Seen or Heard a Word?			
Word	*In Our Class*	*Somewhere Else in School*	*In My Life/In Our Lives*

Copyright material from Barbara R. Blackburn (2025), *Scaffolding for Success: Helping Learners Meet Rigorous Expectations Across the Curriculum*, Routledge

In a specialized content area, such as math, science, social studies, or related areas of learning, it's useful to compare the standard meaning of a word as well as the specialized one.

Term	Standard Definition	Specialized or Technical Meaning	How Do They Connect?

Explore and Apply Through Writing

First, you can ask your students to write a short story, paragraph, or essay using a set of vocabulary. You might also choose to use more creative ways, such as preparing a proposal for a venture capitalist or writing an advertisement for a friend. I've also had success asking students to create an A-to-Z list about a topic. You'll find many of the writing activities in Chapter 6 are to be applicable here.

Another option is to place your students in small groups to create poems about the vocabulary words. I recommend a haiku, the Japanese patterned three-line poem. Line one must include five syllables; line two, seven syllables; and line three, five syllables. It provides an interesting challenge to students to condense the information and present it following the pattern.

> **Middle School Science Sample**
> Beat by beat, it pumps.
> Four chambers give and receive.
> Lifeline in rhythm.

Another way to make vocabulary more memorable is to have students develop concrete poems to help them remember the meaning of the word. Concrete poetry allows your students to be creative and use visuals. This is more motivating to your students who don't always feel successful with language. Since they must use words that describe or define the term or concept in order to create the picture, it is more challenging than it first appears.

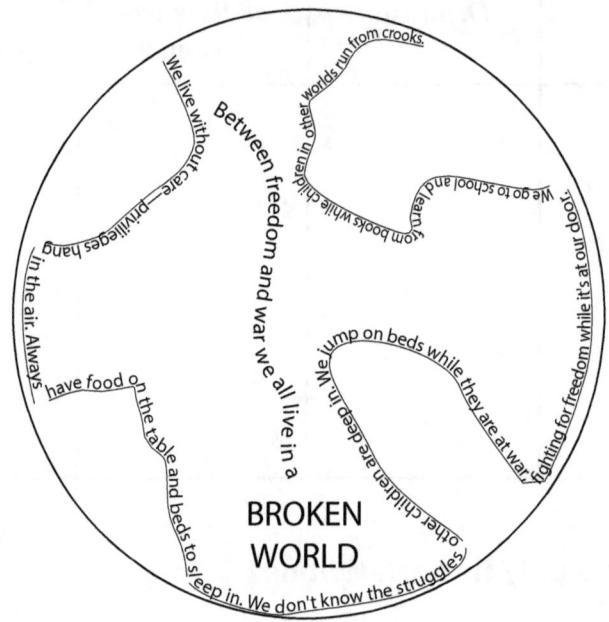

Explore and Apply Through Games

Games are another way to allow students to reinforce, apply, and explore their vocabulary learning. Let's look at four.

> Riddles
> Headband
> Connections
> Dram Slam

One game that is engaging for students is a "What Am I?" riddle. Students use what they know about vocabulary concepts to write a short riddle. When I was at Loris High School, teachers used this idea. Their students created "Who Am I?" and "What Am I?" raps to review content.

> I can show you where things are, but I'm not a tour guide
> I have a scale, but I don't weigh things.
> I contain roads, but I'm not a city.
> I can be on paper or on a phone, but I'm not a shopping list.
> I can show you what is north, south, west, and east, but I'm not a compass.
>
> *Answer: A Map.*

Elementary students also love the riddles. I was recently in a kindergarten classroom. Students created two-line riddles.

> I have four sides that are all the same.
>
> *Answer: A Square.*

Once you teach students how to write riddles, they love to create them and try to stump their classmates. In addition to learning at a higher level, they have fun!

> **Rules for Riddles**
> Riddles are short—no more than five lines.
> The last line is "What am I?" or "Who am I?"
> Lines do not have to rhyme.
> Clues have to be true—or true to the fictional context

During "Headband," former first grade teacher Erin wrote a word on a sentence strip and made it into a headband. First graders in her class gave clues to the person wearing the headband, who guessed the word. All students were involved, and the activity encouraged her students to learn from each other.

James, a middle school drama teacher, points out that his students find the language of Shakespearean plays challenging. For key scenes, students are broken into groups with five acting parts and a group director.

Students identify difficult turns of phrase or specific vocabulary words and make their best educated guess as to meaning. They run lines with one another to improve pronunciation and dramatic reading. The director makes suggestions as to simple stage movements that can be done in the small space at the front of the room. The group discusses appropriate tone, body language, and facial expression. Concerning themselves with the dramatic aspects of presenting to the other three groups more or less forces them to make meaning. Each group takes a turn in a kind of 'drama slam.' They try to outdo the others and get delightfully hammy.

Connections

My new favorite game to use with students is Connections. Created by *The New York Times*, students are provided 16 words. Readers should group them into four sets of four. It is surprisingly challenging, especially since some words might fit into two categories. Let's look at a sample of just two sets of four excerpted from *The New York Times*:

> Canal. Volume. Sound. Quantity.
> Number. Strait. Amount. Channel.

I talked with several high school students, who enjoyed the intricacy of the categories. You can be as simple or complex as you like, but you also want students to discuss the rationale for their categories.

Other Games

Jeopardy
Pictionary
Who Wants to Be a Millionaire
Tic-Tac-Toe
Bingo
Charades
Barrier Crosswords (they are given the word; they write the clues)

Key Ideas

- It's foundational to create a culture that celebrates vocabulary.
- Intentionality enhances your vocabulary instruction.
- Students learn best when they explore and apply vocabulary through reading, word sorts, writing, and games.

 ### Thoughts to Consider

1. What are two or three main points you learned?
2. What is one strategy you would like to implement?
3. What is a question you would like to explore in more depth?

5

Scaffolding Comprehension Across the Subject Areas

Another key aspect of instruction related to scaffolding is comprehension. You'll notice I'm not saying reading, although comprehension is a part of reading. Instead, I'm broadening my focus to comprehension—understanding in all content areas and with all media, whether it is text or visuals. Comprehension can be a major stumbling block in all content areas. When reading texts, students may struggle with the format of informational text, the technical vocabulary, or the denseness of the writing. When analyzing visuals, students may not know how to interpret subtle aspects of the work. And a lack of prior specialized knowledge can be a barrier. In this chapter, we'll focus on four areas of scaffolding that can help your students improve in comprehension.

> Activating Prior Knowledge
> TEACH with Purpose
> Comprehension Strategies
> Matching Rigorous Tasks with Scaffolding Supports

Activating Prior Knowledge

Activating prior knowledge provides a base for learning; therefore, it is a strong scaffolding tool. There are several ways you can activate prior knowledge.

Anticipation Guides

Anticipation guides allow students to state what they know then revisit that after learning. In the first example, students write what they know about a topic then add what they learn from reading two books.

Topic	What I Know	Book One	Book Two

In this sample, younger students draw what they know then revise their drawings after the lesson.

Draw What I Think I Know About the Topic	Revise Your Drawing After the Lesson

They can also be more structured.

Hero Anticipation Guide		
Directions: Please complete the following chart according to your opinions. You will not be graded on your opinions. There is not necessarily one right answer, so answer honestly.		
Agree	**Disagree**	**Statement**
_____	_____	1. Heroes are always courageous.
_____	_____	2. Courage always involves sacrifice.
_____	_____	3. There are many acts of courage in a war.
_____	_____	4. A hero is born that way and shows heroism through his or her actions.
_____	_____	5. A hero is always honest and law-abiding.
_____	_____	6. Someone can be considered a hero only if they win.
_____	_____	7. If a person does something heroic but gets something out of doing it, then she or he is not a hero.
_____	_____	8. A hero is someone who is different than the rest of society.
_____	_____	9. A hero's actions result in the greater good.

Source: Adapted from SpringBoard Curriculum Mathematics Example

Agree/Disagree Before the Lesson	Content	Agree/Disagree After the Lesson
	A right *triangle* can be an *isosceles* triangle.	
	A *right triangle* includes one right angle.	
	A *scalene triangle* is one with all no equal sides.	

K-W-L Charts

Probably the most common method of identifying students' prior knowledge that I see in classrooms today is a K-W-L chart. During a K-W-L activity, you ask the students what they already know about a topic (K) or what they think they know about it. Next, you ask what they want to know (W). Then, you teach the lesson and ask them what they learned (L). You can also add an H—"How Can We Learn This"—to create a K-W-H-L organizer.

K-W-H-L Chart			
K (what I know or think I know)	W (what I want to learn)	H (how I can learn this)	L (what I learned)

One alternative is an adaptation Sarah Lalonde makes in her online guide. She expands to model for science classrooms to a KLEWS. K and L stay the same, then she adds Evidence, what a student Wonders, and any Science vocabulary.

IIQEE

Eric Jensen and LeAnn Nickelsen, in their book *7 Powerful Strategies for In-Depth and Longer-Lasting Learning*, share the IIQEE strategy. It is similar to a K-W-L, but it goes much deeper.

IIQEE Strategy
I think I know the following about the topic . . .
I am sure that I know the following . . .
Questions that I have about the topic (I want to learn) . . .
Experiences that I have had with this topic . . .
Experiences that my friend has had with the topic . . .

A final way to activate prior knowledge is through the "Hot Air Balloon." Students draw a balloon on a piece of paper then write everything they know about a question or topic. Next, students work in groups to determine the "highest" balloon. Groups then post their balloons on the wall, gauging which one is the highest of the class.

Instruction—TEACH with a Purpose

As we discussed in Chapter 2: Planning, scaffolding works best when you plan for it. It is more effective when you teach with a purpose.

Teach Explicitly

It's important to teach explicitly. Brad Witzel, in our book *Rigor for Students for Special Needs*, shares that you may think that explicit instruction is simply standing in front of students and telling them what to learn. But effective explicit instruction is far more complex, with 16 steps.

Steps for Explicit Instruction
1. Focus instruction on critical content
2. Sequence skills logically
3. Task analyze complex skills into smaller steps
4. Design focused lessons

5. Set the expectation to start the lesson
6. Review prior skills
7. Demonstrate stepwise instructions
8. Use clear and concise language
9. Provide examples and nonexamples
10. Provide students guided practice
11. Require frequent responses
12. Monitor student performance closely
13. Provide immediate feedback (corrective or affirmation)
14. Deliver instruction at a brisk pace
15. Connect information across lessons and content
16. Provide abundant time for practice and cumulative review

Source: Archer and Hughes (2011)

While a single lesson rarely incorporates each of these elements, these elements should be considered as a means for intensifying instruction and intervention. This means that, when students in core instruction have increased difficulty in mathematics, more elements would be included in the core instruction. Likewise, intervention settings should incorporate more elements of explicit instruction than core instruction. The following checklist may be used as an internal assessment of the application of the elements of explicit instruction.

Teacher: _____ Date: _____				
Rater: ☐Self ☐Peer ☐Administrator ☐Other				
Class time observed: _____				
Instructional Component	Yes	No	NA	Detail
Lesson content addresses critical content based on the needs of the student				

(continued)

(continued)

Instructional Component	Yes	No	NA	Detail
Skills are sequenced up to this lesson				
Instruction is task analyzed				
Teacher focuses instruction on key areas of the standard and/or math content				
Teachers starts with student expectations and the purpose of the lesson				
Teacher reviews previous concepts at the beginning of the lesson				
Teacher reveals stepwise approach				
Teacher models with clear and concise think aloud language				
Teacher provides multiple examples and at least one non-example of a common error pattern				
Students engage with the teacher and/or other students to solve problems				
Students frequently respond to questions				
Teacher collects formative assessment on students' performance				
Teacher provides immediate corrective feedback				

(*continued*)

(continued)

Instructional Component	Yes	No	NA	Detail
There is little to no down time within the class				
Students independently solve problems				
Teacher concludes lesson with review of daily content and cumulative review				

While a single lesson rarely incorporates each of these elements, you want to include as many as are appropriate.

Extend Their Current Knowledge

As a part of teaching, it's important to help students extend their current knowledge. So, in addition to activating what students already know, provide opportunities for them to move beyond that to new information from the lesson.

Kendra, one of my former graduate students and a former teacher, adjusts the K-W-L strategy into a LINK for her students.

LINK Chart			
L (list everything you know)	*I (inquire about what you want to know)*	*N (now we are going to take notes)*	*K (what do you know now?)*

After they complete the L column individually, her students turn to a partner and share their answers. Then, she leads a short class discussion, charting out what everyone in the class knows about the topic. As she works through the lesson, students finish by writing what they now know (K), and they tear that part off to turn in as they leave her class. This provides her immediate feedback as to what her students learned or didn't learn in class.

It's important to share students' responses with everyone, albeit it in a safe way that doesn't embarrass anyone. That's why I like her method. She starts by allowing each student to write an individual response, so everyone has an opportunity to think about what they know. As Kendra points out, if I'm a student:

> [B]y sharing with a partner, I can feel "safer" in case I'm not right. In the whole class discussion, I'm sharing "our" answers (mine and my partner's), so I don't feel like I'm out on a limb by myself. You could even add another option of sharing with two groups of partners before you share with everyone. However, don't sacrifice the whole class discussion. We all learn more together, and it's a safe guess that someone in my class knows something I don't know. Listening to all responses and charting them out for everyone to see helps me build prior knowledge when I don't have much.

Tech Connection

Technology tools can be an excellent way to help students extend their current knowledge. Each of these digital platforms allows teachers to decide how to push content out to students, utilizing audio and video while creating interactive components. Teachers can use think-aloud strategies, visuals, and hyperlinks to motivate students and make the acquisition of new information much more hands-on so that every student is individually engaged.

NearPod—Nearpod is an online platform that allows teachers to create interactive presentations and push content out to students in real time or as a self-guided activity. Polls, links to external sites, matching activities, drag and drop assessment, etc. . . . are all options to formatively assess students' understanding.

EdPuzzle—Edpuzzle is a video-based platform that enables teachers to use digital files to annotate and deliver lessons to students. Using uploaded videos from YouTube or other sites, it is possible to pause the material being presented to ask questions, provide notes, or use a voiceover as a think aloud to enhance student learning. Students watch at their own pace and answer question prompts to ensure understanding.

ThingLink—ThingLink can be a teaching tool or an assessment tool. Using a visual, teachers can create hotposts on the image that provide links to various digital media files or notes which teach students about the image. This allows for all information to be in one place—on a common image. Students can also use this as a creative way to share the information they've learned about a topic.

Apply to Real Life

Applying learning to real life helps students cement their understanding. Using anchor charts can help students organize their information.

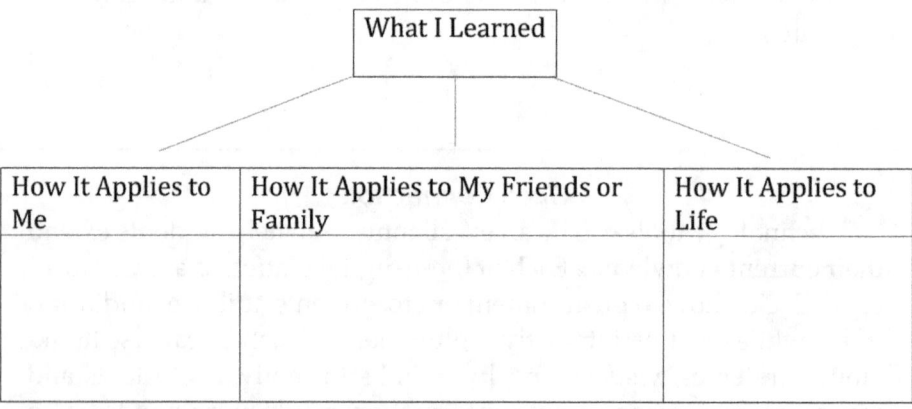

Connect to Broader Knowledge

Another way for students to build connections is to link their knowledge to other knowledge, whether from another topic within your subject area, another subject, or learning at large. Let's look at a graphic organizer that asks students to connect two novels, followed by a chart that asks them to connect multiple sources to broader knowledge.

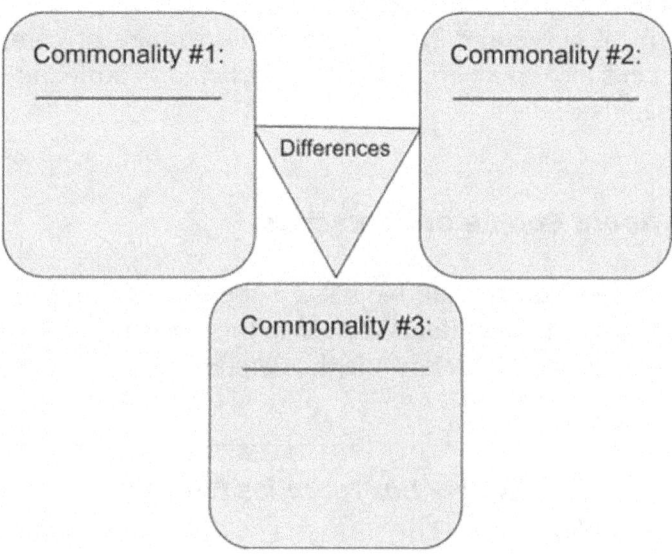

Comparison between Romeo and Juliet vs. West Side Story

World History Holocaust Study	*Date Written/ Published*	*Truths Conveyed about the Holocaust*	*How Did You React to Each Section? What Feelings Were Elicited?*	*How Did this Source Present Historical Facts?*
Assigned research article				
Holocaust survivor speech				
Primary source documents				

Harness New Knowledge Through Activities

Finally, provide opportunities for students to participate in activities for all aspects of learning. I'm providing you with a wide range of activities throughout the book that you can use to help students process understanding.

Comprehension Strategies

In a typical classroom, you'll use a wide range of comprehension strategies. Let's look at a variety that are particularly suited to scaffolding learning to higher levels.

Learning About People or Characters

One way you can help students learn about a person is to use a mystery box. The box includes items related to the person, and as you pull the items out, students try to determine the person.

> **Mystery Box for Julius Caesar:**
> A foot-long ruler
> Brut Cologne (et tu Brutis)
> Caesar salad
> Calendar
> Washington Senators logo
> Dance like an Egyptian (Cleopatra link)

Next, you can use an inside out diagram. Ideal for younger students, they identify characteristics on the outside of the character, then on the inside, for a deeper character analysis.

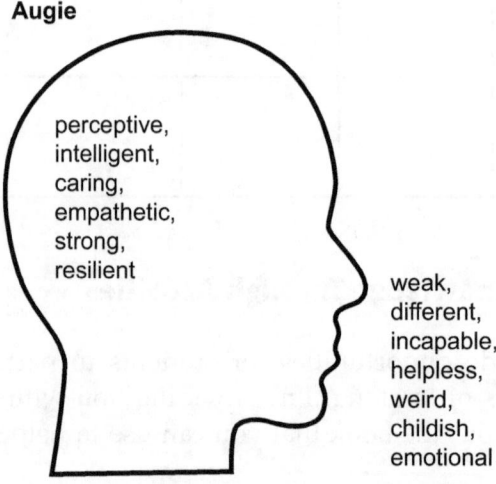

Augie

Inside: perceptive, intelligent, caring, empathetic, strong, resilient

Outside: weak, different, incapable, helpless, weird, childish, emotional

88 ◆ Scaffolding for Success

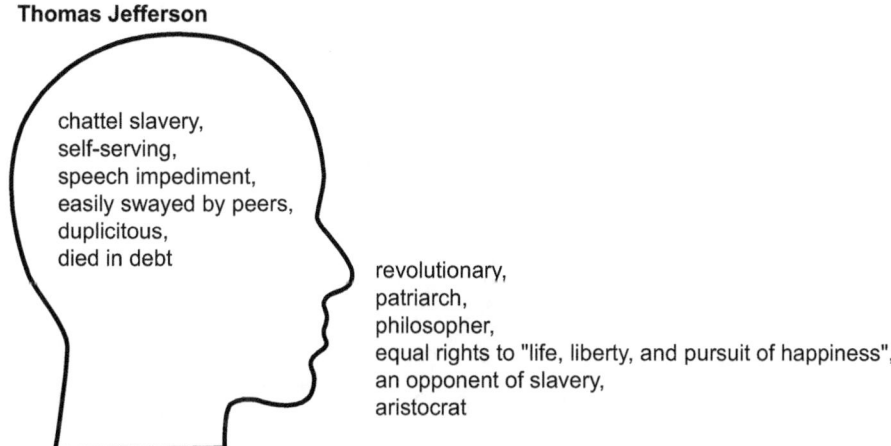

Flesh It Out

Let's look at a fun visual to help students go deeper with a topic. Flesh It Out, originally created by Janet Allen, requires an analysis of a prominent historical figure or character in a novel. Rather than simply writing basic information about a person or character, students are expected to research and describe more specific information, which allows them to create a finished product with more complexity. It's also ideal for processing math word problems.

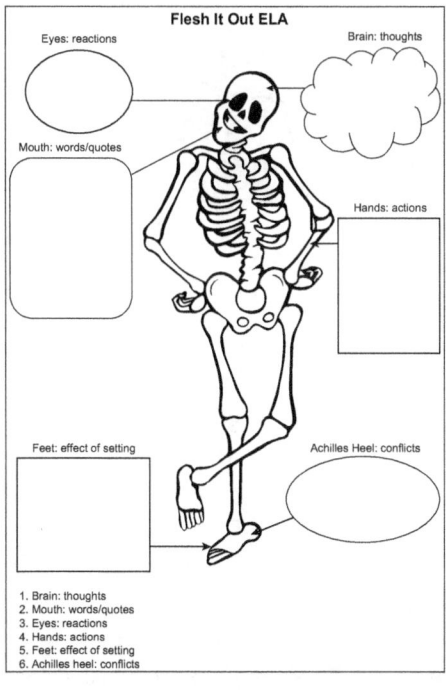

Copyright material from Barbara R. Blackburn (2025), *Scaffolding for Success: Helping Learners Meet Rigorous Expectations Across the Curriculum*, Routledge

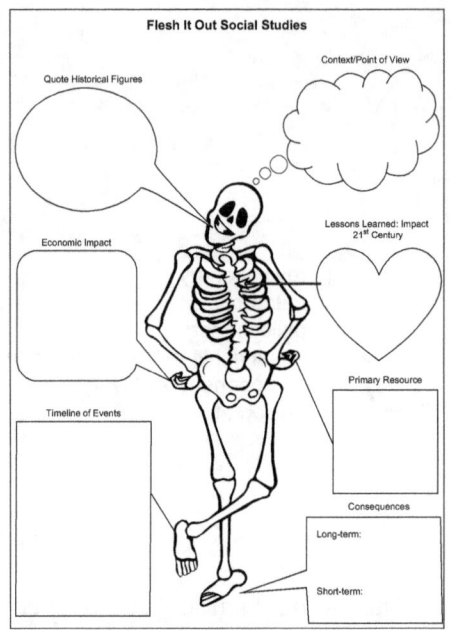

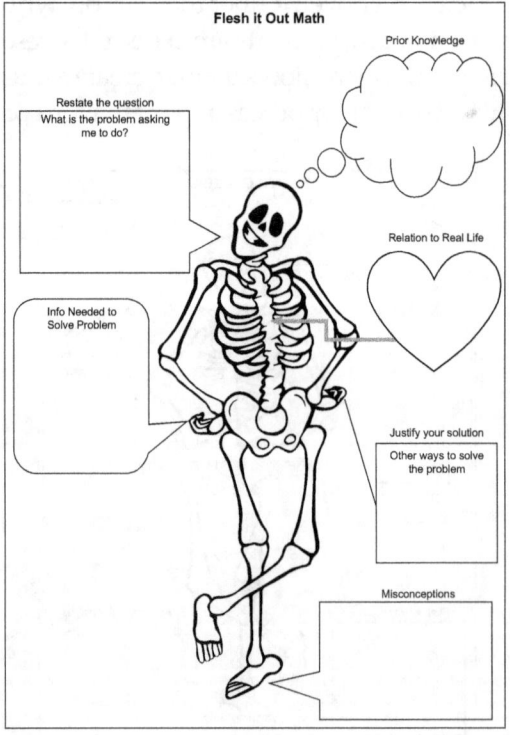

Copyright material from Barbara R. Blackburn (2025), *Scaffolding for Success: Helping Learners Meet Rigorous Expectations Across the Curriculum*, Routledge

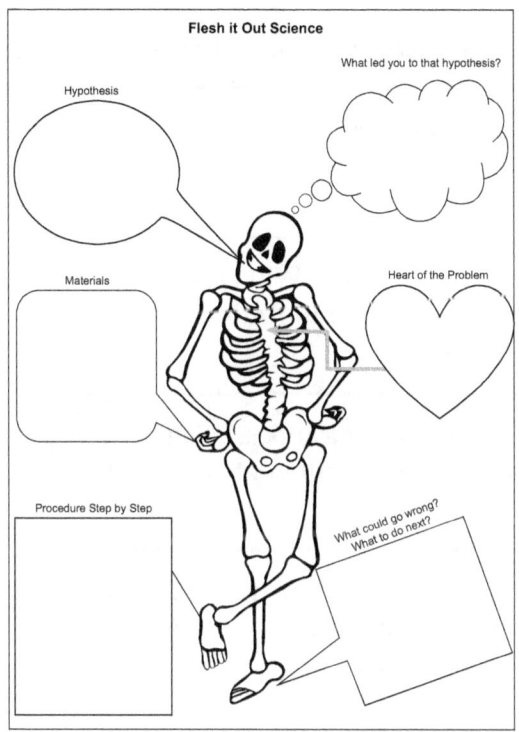

Understanding the Textbook

Years ago, I worked for Scott Foresman, which published textbooks. One of the things I remember was hearing a speaker talk about the difficulty students have reading textbooks. I was also interested in the strategies the company used to help students better understand what they are reading. For examples, they chose not to divide words at the end of a line or divide a sentence from the bottom of one page to the top of the next page. If that happens, it breaks a student's comprehension. I never thought of something that simple making a difference to learning.

Whether you are asking students to read a portion of text, you will also want to model your thinking. It's important to provide a guide. Otherwise, students won't know what to look for. These can be detailed or more general. If you blend a think-aloud with study guide notes, it is very effective for students to use in group, partner, or individual work. Guide-o-Ramas combine a study guide with your modeling.

Copyright material from Barbara R. Blackburn (2025), *Scaffolding for Success: Helping Learners Meet Rigorous Expectations Across the Curriculum*, Routledge

3rd Grade Reading Guide on Volcanoes	
Based on the title, what questions do you hope to have answered in this short informative text?	
Take a look at the image on p. 1. What can you learn about the location of the world's volcanoes from this image?	
Read the section "Types of Volcanoes." Can you draw and label the three different types of volcanic structures?	
After reading the third paragraph, define the word magma in your own words.	Magma is . . .

"The Invention and History of the Printing Press"	
What do you already know about the printing press before you begin reading?	
Read the first two sections. What role do monasteries play in the earliest days of literature and texts?	
Click on the link *Earliest Manuscripts*. Skim through the information on religious manuscripts and secularization of book production. Summarize the evolution of the earliest "books" of the 3rd–7th century in two the sentences.	
Go back to the main site and read the section The Invention of the Printing Press. What was Gutenburg's inspiration for this invention?	
Create a visual timeline of significant developments in printing between the 1430s and 1700.	

Suzanne Manz created THIEVES to help students organize a chapter of a textbook.

Area	What I Learned
Title	
Headings	
Introduction	
Every First Sentence in a Paragraph	
Visuals and Vocabulary	
End-of-Chapter Questions	
Summary	

Suzanne Liff Manz, The Reading Teacher, Volume 55, February 5, 2022.

Understanding the Text Across Subject Areas

It is crucial for students of all ages to use active reading skills when interacting with and understanding content area texts. The following chart outlines the ways in which students should be engaging with the texts in your classroom: by making connections to what they already know, asking clarifying questions to gauge their own understanding, making inferences, drawing conclusions, visualizing, and synthesizing information.

	Math	Science	Social Studies	Language Arts
Make connections	How do fractions connect to decimals?	How would endangered animals connect to the food chain of an ecosystem?	What are the connections between the militant groups the Taliban and Boko Haram?	How does the oppression occurring in our novel connect to current events in Afghanistan?
Ask questions	What information is relevant in this word problem?	Am I understanding the process of photosynthesis?	Does it make sense to me how electoral votes impact an election?	What are this character's true motives?
Make inferences and draw conclusions	Based on the distributive property, I should be able to multiple this factor with each number inside the parentheses to simplify the equation.	From the text on chemical changes, I can infer that substances are undergoing changes at the molecular level.	After reading Patrick Henry's words, I can infer that his persuasive rhetoric had an instant impact on colonists' view of independence from the British.	This conflict appears to be a pivotal moment in influencing the plot based on the way it is impacting the protagonist.

(continued)

(continued)

	Math	Science	Social Studies	Language Arts
Visualize	When working with factions, can I visualize the numerator in relationship to the denominator (three cookies over ten cookies)?	As I'm reading about the water cycle, can I picture it in my head?	Picture Washington crossing the Delaware to help relate to this historical event.	I can picture characters as they interact with one another to internalize their behaviors and personalities.
Synthesize	Understanding exponents and knowing the distributive property will help me understand order of operations.	By understanding the law of conservation of mass and using what I've learned about reaction types, I can better understand what the text is teaching me about chemical processes.	Considering what the text is saying about the Mayan social structure, architectural achievements, and intellect in mathematics, it's easier to understand how their civilization flourished.	I can use the connotative diction and allusions throughout the poem to fully grasp the poet's perspective.

Source: Adapted and expanded from: Fogelberg, E., Skaalinder, C., Satz, P., Hiller, B., Bernstein, L., & Vitantonio, S. (2008). *Integrating literacy and math.* New York: Guilford Press.

Electronic Texts

Online reading tends to be shallower and more scattered. This is due, in part, to the variety of links that entice students to click on new pages and explore more and more information, which may or may not be related to the original information. There are three steps students should take when reading web pages.

> **3 Steps**
> Focus on the main text
> Think before you click
> Take notes

Videos and Visuals

Videos and other visuals can help students process information, or they may provide information. Whatever the purpose, there are several ways to support comprehension of visuals.

If students are looking at a graph, it's important that they pay attention to the title of the visual, titles of the x-axis and y-axis, column headings, and other text on the graph. Then, they'll compare and analyze the data, such as the bars or pictures. Once they have broken down the aspects, they can analyze the information.

Perhaps students are evaluating political cartoons. Analyzing irony, exaggeration, sarcasm, and symbolism are all parts of evaluation.

Read-Write-Think provides an excellent lesson for teaching analysis of political cartoons: www.readwritethink.org/classroom-resources/lesson-plans/analyzing-purpose-meaning-political.

Guide-o-Rama for Videos

In addition to using a guide-o-rama with text, you can use it with videos, especially if you want students to view it outside of your classroom.

Guide-O-Rama	
Ratios (https://youtu.be/UxWsY59NVgc)	
Time #	*Reading Tip*
0 seconds	What do you already know about ratios? Before I watch a video, I also write down what I'm confused about or what I want to learn.
15 seconds	How does the tutor define ratios? How does it compare to your thoughts? For me, sometimes it doesn't match, so I know I need to pay extra attention to the video.
51 seconds	The first time I watched this, I was a little confused because writing a ratio looks exactly like writing a fraction. Did this confuse you?
1:40	Stop and think for a minute. Is this making sense? If it is confusing, you might want to back up the video now and re-watch it. I've found that it helps me to stop when I don't understand a step rather than waiting until the end.

You may choose to use a guide that is less structured, which requires students to narrow down the information from the source.

Broader Viewing Guide

Viewing Guide for_____		
What are the key points in the video?	What examples are given for each of the main points?	What questions do you have?
What is the most important thing you learned from the video?		

Scaffolding Comprehension Across the Subject Areas ◆ 97

Points of View

Still another way to help students think about a topic from a variety of perspectives is through the use of Thinking Hats (DeBono, 1999). The process provides six different ways of viewing or discussing information and is helpful anytime you want students to look at something through different lenses.

Thinking Hats

The White Hat calls for information known or needed. "The facts, just the facts."

The Yellow Hat symbolizes brightness and optimism. Under this hat, you explore the positives and probe for value and benefit.

The Black Hat is judgment—the devil's advocate or why something may not work. Spot the difficulties and dangers—where things might go wrong. Probably the most powerful and useful of the hats but a problem if overused.

The Red Hat signifies feelings, hunches, and intuition. When using this hat, you can express emotions and feelings and share fears, likes, dislikes, loves, and hates.

The Green Hat focuses on creativity—the possibilities, alternatives, and new ideas. It's an opportunity to express new concepts and new perceptions.

The Blue Hat is used to manage the thinking process. It's the control mechanism that ensures the Six Thinking Hats® guidelines are observed.

Source: https://www.debonogroup.com/services/core-programs/six-thinking-hats/

As a side note, I have spoken with many teachers who have pointed out that the color of the black hat may be perceived as negative by some students. I prefer to change this to a purple hat to avoid any issues. Also, if you google, you will find other hats people have designed such as an orange hat for communication, a gray hat for consequences, or a gold hat for diversity.

Elaine Adkins-McEwan has developed the *7 Thinking Hats of Skilled Readers* that you may find useful. Her full description provides additional information.

Hat	Tasks
Graduate	Has prior knowledge
Detective	Searches for clues to solve a mystery
Taxi Driver	Knows when he or she is lost and corrects course
Police Officer	Asks questions to get to the bottom of the story
Explorer	Has time to visit only the most important places
Reporter	Concisely sticks to the facts
Artist	Creates images to make something come alive

Source: McEwan-Adkins, E. (2016). *The 7 thinking hats of skilled readers.* Learning Sciences International.

Thinking Like a Disciplinarian

As a part of preparing students for college and careers, it is good practice to teach students how to navigate specialized content. Additionally, thinking analytically from the perspective of varied content areas is reflected throughout most national and state standards. Many of us became teachers in our chosen content areas because we enjoyed learning the content, but how well did we truly understand the content? Abbigail Armstrong, co-author of *Rigor in the Math and Science Classroom*, remembers the first time her mathematical thinking was challenged. She immediately shut down but, thanks to a persistent teacher who believed she could do it, she became a better mathematics student and a better mathematics teacher. She learned to question her own thinking, reflect, and process her thinking like a mathematician.

From a scaffolding perspective, teaching students to think from their discipline perspective is essential for them to become proficient in the areas.

> **How Mathematicians Think**
> - Recognize that all reasoning depends on assumptions.
> - Believe you could be wrong.
> - Value intuition and ideas.
> - Question numbers.
> - Model things.

Source: Josh Bernoff, co-author of *Groundswell* and other books

> **How Scientists Think**
> - Ask many questions, do your research, and formulate a hypothesis.
> - Make predictions (guess with a purpose).
> - Create and carry out experiments to test your hypothesis and predictions.
> - Analyze your data and check your assumptions.
> - Draw data-based conclusions and share them with others.

Source: Adapted from www.wikihow.com/Think-Like-a-Scientist

> **How Historians Think**
> - Wonder about how people in the past have viewed their world.
> - Use primary source artifacts and texts to learn about past people groups.
> - Analyze cause and effect. How have the decisions and behaviors of past civilizations impacted cultures and societies today?
> - Research theories and be curious about the interconnectedness of societies.
> - Evaluate significant decisions that have changed the course of history.

Matching Rigorous Tasks With Scaffolding Supports

Finally, let's match some scaffolded supports with rigorous tasks. What you'll notice is that I'm not suggesting you change the tasks. Rather, you chunk or help students focus their learning to complete the task. Here, I'm providing sample graphic organizers you could use. Of course, modeling the task is also important for struggling learners.

Middle School Science

Students identify an issue or a situation related to science, such as the proposal to add solar panels to the roof of the school or creating a school garden. Research the issue, including benefits and disadvantages, and identify any impact on the school, students, teachers, or anyone else interested in the decision. Finally, design and present a plan to convince teachers and parents of their position and any recommended changes, with specific evidence supporting their decision.

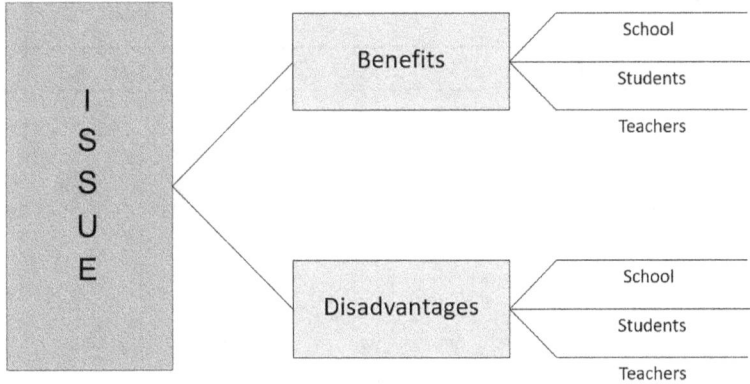

Volume in Elementary School Math and Science

You must figure out how much cereal will fit into a cereal box without measuring the box. Three responses have been provided and you must decide which makes more sense. Illustrate or write how you figured out which response made more sense. Justify or support your reasoning as to why the others did not make sense.

Problem	*This Makes Sense Because . . .*	*This Doesn't Make Sense Because . . .*
1		
2		
3		

Close Reading Research and Writing with K-1

After reading our book about ants, let's read "The Queen Ant's Birthday" and look for evidence of the different types of ant characters. Who are the worker bees and guard bees, and what do they do for Queen Ant? How does the queen function like the queen bee in our nonfiction book? How do these bees live in community? What can we learn about living in community with one another? In addition to using evidence from the texts, provide real-life examples to support your responses.

Source: *Idea adapted from ReadingA-Z.com

Worker Bees	*Guard Bees*

⬇ ⬇

What They Do For Queen Bee	*What They Do For Queen Bee*

102 ◆ Scaffolding for Success

Exploring Perspectives/Dinner Parties (Social Studies)

Imagine a dinner party with esteemed guests such as Stalin, Truman, Churchill, and Eleanor Roosevelt. Using your knowledge of the Yalta, Potsdam, and Tehran conferences in the 1940's, write a script in which these historical figures converse about their different views of what the world would look like after World War II. Choose a character, and role play this scenario, keeping the original integrity of your guest intact. At your dinner party, be sure to include what each historical figure would say about the state of society today.

	Key Things They Would Say	*What the World Would Look Like After WW2*	*What They Would Say About Our World*
Stalin			
Truman			
Churchill			
E. Roosevelt			

Students move through an art gallery of work created by their classmates. Each student chooses one piece of art and writes a short critique. The critique must include the student's opinion of the artwork, support of the opinion based on the lesson taught by the teacher and the student's own experiences, and recommendations for improvement.

Critique		
My Opinion	*Evidence From Lesson*	*Evidence From My Experiences*
Recommendations		

Key Ideas

- Activating prior knowledge is foundational to understanding.
- Intentionally teaching comprehension skills is more effective.
- Using a variety of comprehension skills helps students learn in all content areas.
- Scaffolding allows you to expect students to work at rigorous levels.

Thoughts to Consider

1. What are two or three main points you learned?
2. What is one strategy you would like to implement?
3. What is a question you would like to explore in more depth?

6

Scaffolding Writing in the Content Areas

Why is writing important? Because it is reflective of thinking, and it is a critical life skill. If you want students to think at higher levels, then provide opportunities for them to write. One of the most important scaffolding tools in writing, as in our other areas, is modeling. In *Writing Science Right*, Sue Neuen and Elizabeth Tebeaux suggest providing an outline for students to create and organize their writing.

Helping Students Create and Organize Their Writing

1. **Collecting and Grouping Information**
2. **Planning Content Development according to Four Reader-Friendly Text Patterns:**
   A. Topical Arrangement
   B. Reports Designed for Specific Reader Needs
   C. Chronological Arrangement
3. **Strategies for Developing Content**
   A. Partitions
   B. Definitions
   C. Questions
   D. Headings

Modeling Deconstruction

Deconstructing a text and writing task into different elements specific to that mode of writing is powerful way to visibly break down writing. This helps students see the writing broken down into smaller, more manageable pieces that can be reconstructed with a variety of similar prompts.

For example, deconstructing the elements of an expository paragraph is necessary in all content areas. Students can think of this as a recipe that needs certain ingredients every time– no matter the subject or grade level.

Expository responses:

Topic sentence that restates the question→

Evidence to support the topic (from text or data)→

Elaboration/Explanation of how the evidence supports the topic→

Transition words/phrase if necessary to include more evidence and explanation→

Conclusion sentence

The same process can be used in other areas.

Scientific lab responses: a) definition of the problem b) background information c) hypothesis d) observations e) testing procedures f) conclusions	Speech analysis: S = who is the speaker? O = what is the occasion? A = who is the intended audience? P = what is the purpose? S = what is the subject? Tone = what is his or her tone and how does it impact the message?

By teaching students to look for elements specific to different genres, they will more readily be able to use the elements when constructing their own text in that mode of writing.

Modeling the Purpose

It's particularly important to model and provide examples for students depending on the purpose of writing. Maria Grant, Diane Lapp, and Marisol Thayre, in *Teaching Writing from Content Classroom to Career*, note there are a variety of purposes in content areas. First, you express and reflect, such as in a blog entry or poetry. Next, you can inform and explain in a report or presentation. Third, you might evaluate and judge in a critique or product review. Fourth, you can analyze and interpret in a data analysis or research project. Finally, you might take a stand or propose a solution in an editorial or social media campaign. Providing a mentor text is an excellent way to model these purposes.

	Grades K-6	*Grades 7–12*
Express and Reflect	◆ *Dogku* by Andrew Clements ◆ *Street Music: City Poems* by Arnold Adoff ◆ *Where the Sidewalk Ends* by Shel Silverstein ◆ *Silver Seeds* by Paul Paolilli and Dan Brewer ◆ *Shaking Things Up* by Susan Hood ◆ *All the Wild Wonders* edited by Wendy Cooling	◆ https://alwaysabbynoel.blogspot.com/ ◆ https://furreekatt.blogspot.com/ ◆ https://cultivatingcriticalreaders.com/mentor-texts-for-poetry/ ◆ *If I Never Forever Endeavor* by Holly Meade ◆ *Where I'm From* by George Ella High School ◆ *The Hill We Climb* by Amanda Gorman ◆ Jason Reynold's *Long Way Down*
Inform and Explain	◆ https://wonderopolis.org/ ◆ https://kids.nationalgeographic.com/ ◆ https://newsforkids.net/ ◆ www.timeforkids.com ◆ www.dogonews.com/	◆ www.nationalgeographic.com/magazine/ ◆ *The Code Book: The Science of Secrecy from Ancient Egypt to Quantum Cryptography* by Simon Singh ◆ *Eye to Eye: How Animals See the World* by Steve Jenkins ◆ *Tires Are Saving Us—and Killing Us, Too* by Tim Stevens for TheVerge.com ◆ *Surgeons Perform Second Pig Heart Transplant, Trying to Save a Dying Man* by Lauren Neergaard for APNews.com ◆ *'Wiretaps on Wheels': How Your Car Is Collecting and Selling Your Personal Data* by Frank Bajak for the *Los Angeles Times*

(continued)

(continued)

	Grades K–6	*Grades 7–12*
Evaluate and Judge	♦ https://luckylittlelearners.com/14-mentor-texts-to-introduce-opinion-writing/	♦ *Everything's an Argument* by Andrea A. Lunsford and John J. Ruszkiewicz ♦ Examples of book reviews: ♦ www.ttms.org/PDFs/12%20Book%20Talk%20v001%20(Full).pdf
Analyze and Interpret	♦ Using student mentor work is most appropriate	♦ www.smithsonianmag.com ♦ www.dogonews.com/ ♦ www.commonlit.org ♦ www.nytimes.com/column/learning-mentor-texts
Take a Stand or Propose a Solution	♦ *Jabari Jumps* by Gaia Cornwall ♦ *The Brownstone* by Paula Scher ♦ *Why Should I Recycle?* Jen Green	♦ *The Book of Bad Arguments* by Ali Almossawi ♦ *Attention, Students: Put Your Laptops Away* by James Doubek ♦ *Is it Actually Smart to Sit Still?* by Hannah Amell ♦ "Ain't I a Woman?" by Sojourner Truth, delivered 1851, Women's Convention, Akron, Ohio ♦ "The Destructive Male" by Elizabeth Cady Stanton, delivered 1868, Women's Suffrage Convention, Washington, D.C.

Modeling With Three Guidelines/Choices

When I was a teacher, I suggested three simple guidelines for students. I described three choices an effective writer makes.

> Brief over Wordy
> Simple over Complex
> Specific over Vague

First, don't use ten words to describe something when five will do. Wordiness leads to repetition, which isn't necessary. Next, choose a simple, understandable explanation over one that is complex and confusing. Finally, be specific rather than vague, pointing out there are three parts rather than some parts.

	Choose...	*Over...*
Brief Over Wordy	Numbers are important, but so is the process you use.	I think it's important to consider that, when you are thinking about math, it's not just the numbers that matter; in fact, it's what you do with the numbers instead.
Simple Over Complex	Democracy is a political system that incorporates participation by the general population, representation for all, and protection of individual rights.	Democracy is a multifaceted political system that encompasses a range of key components, each contributing to the intricate tapestry of governance characterized by popular participation, representation, and the protection of individual rights. The complexity of democracy arises from the dynamic interplay among these components, fostering a system that aims to balance power, promote civic engagement, and safeguard fundamental freedoms.
Specific Over Vague	Four scientists explored...	Some scientists explored...

Purposes of Writing in the Classroom

There are four ways to use writing in your classroom and ways to scaffold writing within each of those.

> Writing to Activate Learning
> Writing to Process Learning
> Writing to Demonstrate Learning
> Writing to Apply Learning

Writing to Activate Learning

The first way to use writing in your classroom is to activate learning or determine the background knowledge your students have about what you are teaching. We looked at KWHL in Chapter 5, but it's important enough I want to revisit it as a writing strategy.

KWL-KWHL

Probably the most common method of identifying students' prior knowledge that I see in classrooms today is a K-W-L chart which we discussed earlier. During a K-W-L activity, you ask the students what they already know about a topic (K) or what they think they know about it. Next, you ask what they want to know (W). Then, you teach the lesson and ask them what they learned (L). You can also add an H—How Can We Learn This to create a K-W-H-L organizer. This allows each student to share but also to learn from other students.

K-W-H-L Chart			
K (what I know or think I know)	W (what I want to learn)	H (how I can learn this)	L (what I learned)

Footsteps

A creative way to ask students what they know about learning is to place paper footsteps around the room. Students write what they know, one word, phrase, or topic per step. Then, students can pick up the steps and organize them by what they say. This process activates students' knowledge and learning.

Carousels

Carousels are a bit more structured. Rather than asking students to write or draw anything they know, there are posters around the room, each with a word, phrase, or sentence. Students write what they know about the prompt on the poster, then those are used to begin your class. You can have students simply write what they know on the posters, or you can use post-it notes. I like post-it notes because I can pull a poster and rearrange the notes to show how many students agree about a point. I find this reinforces students' confidences, especially when they see that others agree with them.

Anticipation Guides

In Chapter 5, we discussed the use of anticipation guides. An alternative is to have students create their own anticipation guides. As a starting point, you can give them a topic, and they can write three to five things they know or think they know about the topic. Then, working with a partner, they can confirm or correct the items.

Topic:	
What I Know or Think I Know	*Confirm or Correct*

Version for Younger Learners		
What I Know or Think I Know	☺	☹

Writing to Process Learning

Writing is also useful for students to process their learning. One of the easiest ways to do this is with graphic organizers. Whether you use a simple Venn Diagram to compare and contrast two items or a more complex mind map, graphic organizers help students organize and develop their thoughts. Keep in mind that, with younger students, you may want to adapt an organizer or use it as an anchor chart.

Circle Map

A circle map is designed for students to write what they know about a topic. The topic goes in the middle circle, and students write related words in the outer circle. If they aren't sure or if a word doesn't belong, it goes outside the circles.

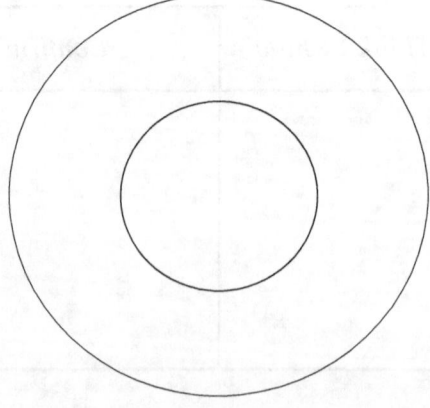

Spider Map

A bit more complicated is a spider map, which can be basic, with related words, or more complex, with related words and descriptors.

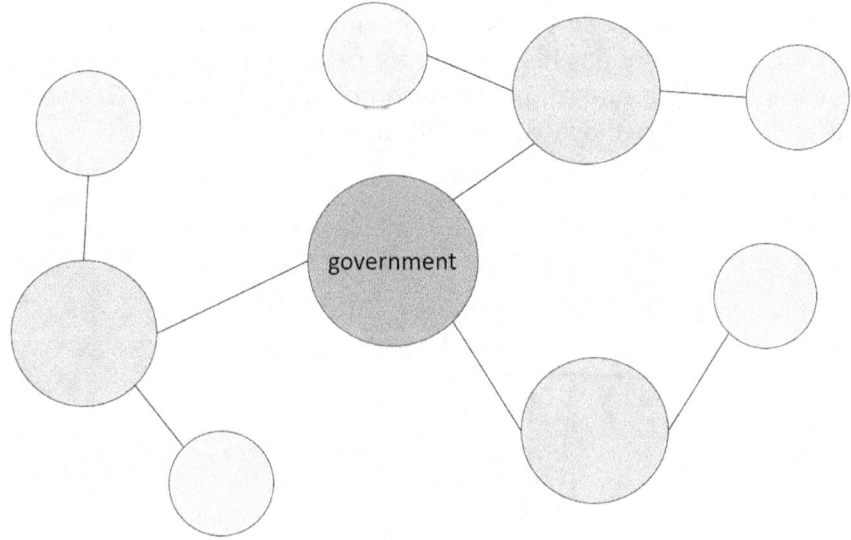

Lotus Diagram

A Lotus Diagram is helpful when you need to process topics and subtopics, so it is especially useful for middle and secondary students. You can make it more structured with multiple blocks, or more open with fewer boxes.

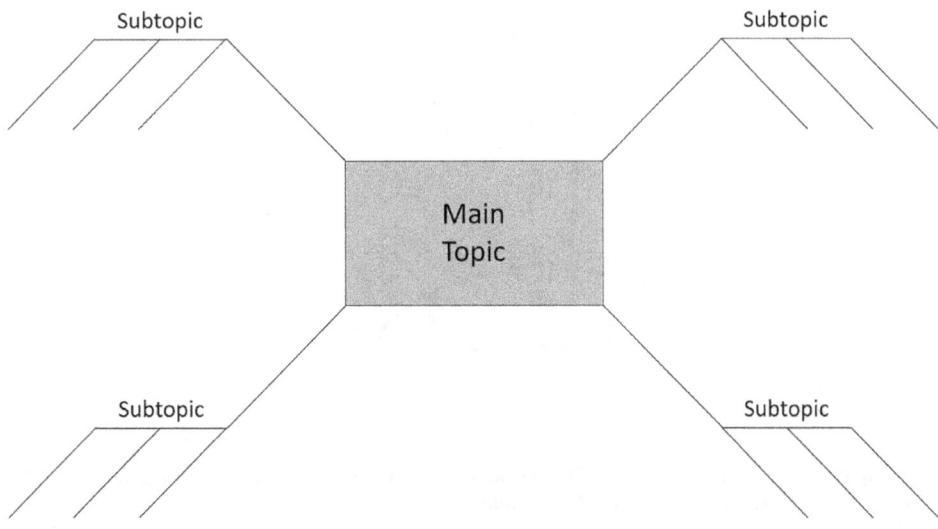

Fishbone

A different organizer that I found particularly helpful was the fishbone. The fishbone graphic organizer is used to explore the aspects of a complex topic. It is particularly helpful if you have one single, complicated topic and then need to detail more information on ideas, examples, or attributes. The fishbone helps students focus, monitor their comprehension, and organize information as you complete the organizer. It also helps them see gaps where they need to find more information.

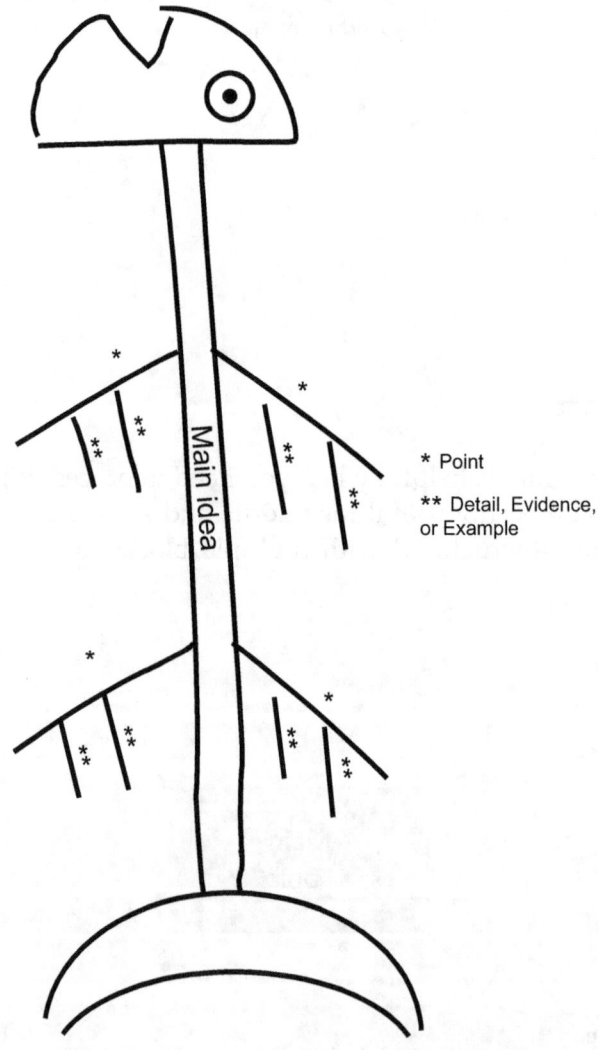

* Point
** Detail, Evidence, or Example

Copyright material from Barbara R. Blackburn (2025), *Scaffolding for Success: Helping Learners Meet Rigorous Expectations Across the Curriculum*, Routledge

Five-Point Star and Chair

Another graphic organizer is a five-point star. Students can write their main point in the middle of the star and examples or evidence on the points. What is interesting is how helpful a simple diagram is. Something like a star helps students visualize what is in their head.

I used a similar metaphor when I was teaching. If students were making a point, such as why a type of government was best, I said their main point was the seat of a chair. Then, their pieces of supporting information were the legs of the chair. If they only had one example, they had a wobbly chair. Ideally, they should have four legs.

Venn Diagram

If you'd like to compare and contrast, a standard Venn Diagram is effective.

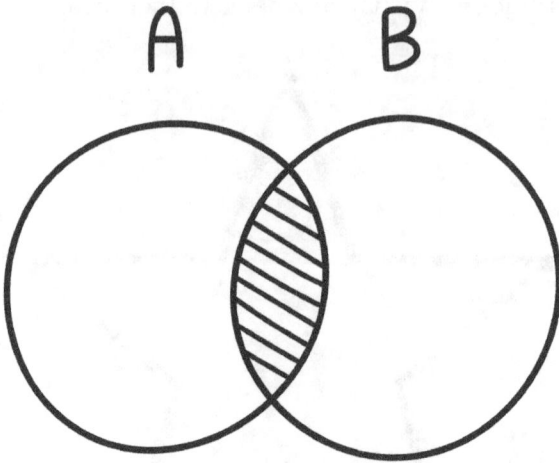

If you'd prefer, you can use a more complex version, comparing three topics or books.

PERSIA

In my book, *Rigor in the 6–12 English/Language Arts and Social Studies Classroom,* Melissa Miles and I provided a PERSIA graphic for high school students. It was designed to look at the political, economic, religious, social, intellectual, and area (geographic) aspects of an event.

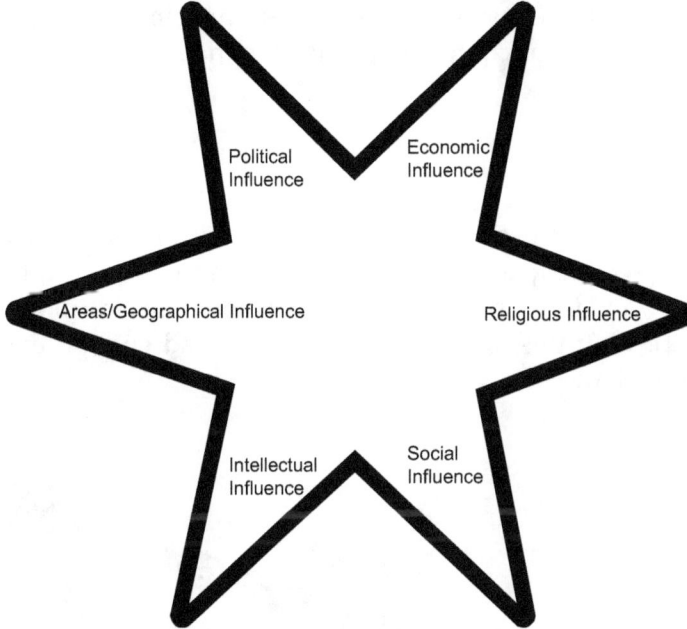

Alan Hosley, an academic content lead in Georgia, redesigned the graphic using circles so his students could see the connections in a different way.

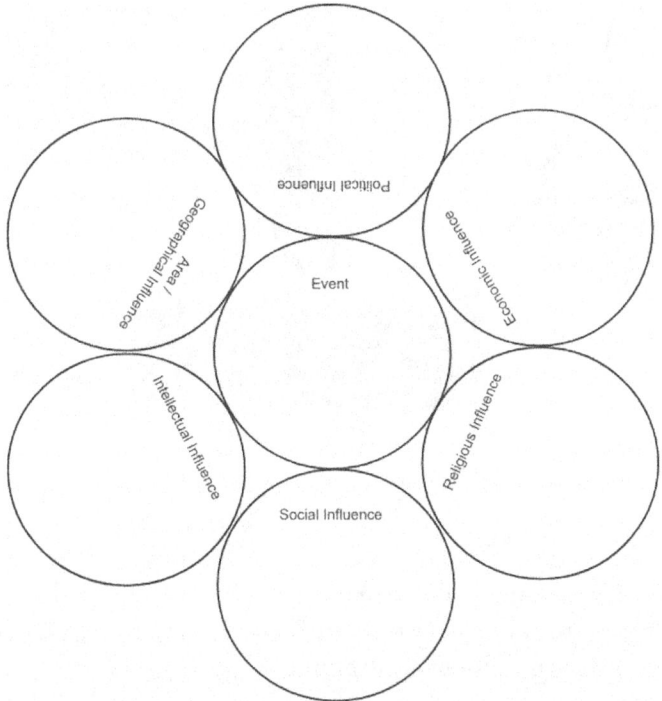

Created by Alan Hosley, Academic Content Lead

You might also consider using something similar to overlapping Olympic Circles if your content lends itself to that.

Scale

Another option I used with my students with persuasive writing or debates was a graphic organizer of a scale. On the base, students wrote their opinion, and they "stacked" their points on each side of the scale (for and against). With this, they could see if they had enough evidence for their point of view.

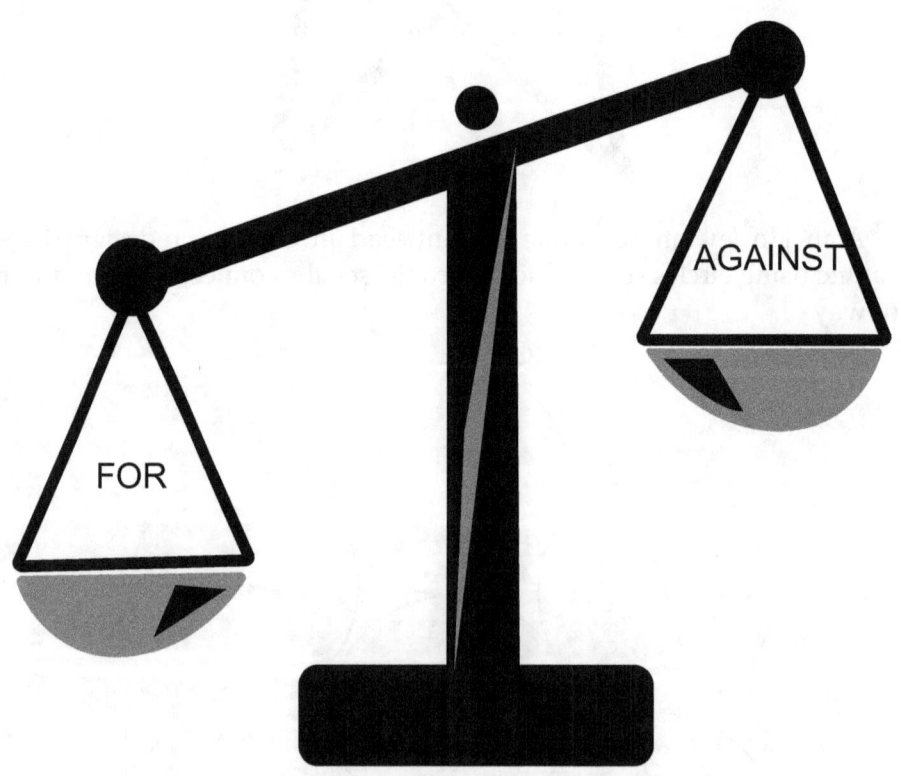

Debates

Some students needed more structure when crafting debates. In that case, individual students or groups can use a graphic organizer like the one that follows to plan their arguments.

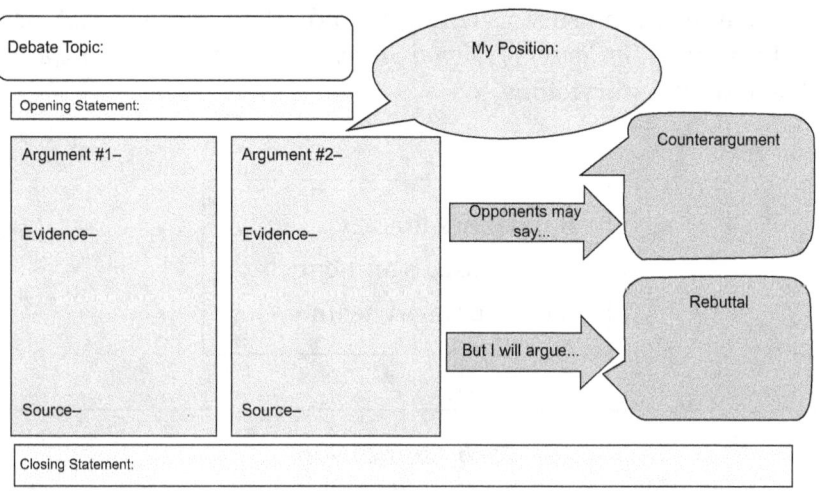

Storyboarding

I find it effective to teach sequencing of events or a process through storyboarding. In a science classroom, I ask students to brainstorm ideas of different steps that might occur during an experiment, either drawing or writing each idea on a separate sticky note. They can reorder their steps based on what actually works during the experiment, adding in any steps they may have left out.

In writing, students can plan an essay or research paper using this process. After they write their ideas and research, students can order and reorder the ideas by rearranging the sticky notes. You can also simply use a template (as follows). I explained to my students that this is a simple version of storyboarding, which is how Walt Disney planned his movies.

Copyright material from Barbara R. Blackburn (2025), *Scaffolding for Success: Helping Learners Meet Rigorous Expectations Across the Curriculum*, Routledge

You may want to use storytelling with digital tools. Michael Hernandez, in his article, *The Power of Digital Storytelling*, points out there are three benefits to digital storytelling.

> It redefines literacy.
> It emphasizes authenticity.
> It discourages cheating.

Tech Connection

You can also use a variety of technology sources for storyboarding. For example, sites such as www.timeline.com, storyboardthat.com, and www.linoit.com allow students to create their own storyboards electronically. Another option is to have students choose from a set of photos online (be sure to screen the photos in advance) to use as a basis for their storyboard. There are also some programs that will allow students to organize their photos and record their story via audio. Capcut is a video tool that could be a useful tool to help younger students record their stories with visuals and audio.

Paragraph Frame

A paragraph frame is also useful as students are getting started. For example, if I want my upper elementary students to analyze an experiment, I may provide a starting point.

> **Simple Science Prompt**
> The purpose of my experiment was . . .
> I observed . . .
> That meant . . .

Prompt: How does Deborah Ellis use symbolism, characters, and conflict to reveal a theme in *The Breadwinner*?

Authors often leave lasting impressions on their readers by revealing a universal truth throughout their stories. _____,
(title of story, italicized and capitalized)
written by _____,
uncovers the
(author's name)
theme that _____.
(your thematic statement, **not** just a word)
This life lesson can be seen through the characters, conflicts, and symbols the author uses.
To begin with, _____'s character _____
(Include textual evidence from a **CHARACTER** that learns or teaches the theme)
_____.
These actions/words show the theme by _____
_____.
(Explain how the evidence you just gave proves your theme idea)
Secondly, this life lesson can be revealed through conflict. _____
_____
_____.
(Choose evidence [no exact quote needed] from a **CONFLICT** that demonstrates the theme)
In this scene, the theme is brought to life by _____
_____.
(explain how the evidence you just gave proves your theme)
Finally, the author uses _____ as a symbol that points
(Choose a SYMBOL we have discussed in class)
toward the theme. _____.
(Discuss the SYMBOL—**exact quote**—that reveals the theme)
Using symbolism, the author communicates the lesson that
_____.
(explain how the evidence you just gave proves your theme idea)
Deborah Ellis cleverly uses her characters, conflicts, and symbols to reveal a life lesson: _____
_____
_____.
(reword your theme)

Reflective Journal

Former teacher Kendra used journals with her students. She asked students to continually reflect on their learning in their *daybooks*, which are simple bound notebooks. Then, she asked them to write a reflection on their learning at the end of the 9 weeks. Some wrote about specific content they learned; others of her students reflected on how they learned.

> "Over this quarter, I've learned many things. One thing I've learned is teachers mean business and don't take kindly to slacking. I found that out the hard way. Another thing is that if you take the time to listen, teachers have a lot of helpful tips for passing the school year."
>
> *Justin, end of first nine weeks*
>
> "Something else that I learn [sic] would be about text organizers such as title, headings, caption/photograph, sidebars, and tags. Text organizers were not that confusing. At first, I was getting tags and headings mixed up, but shortly I begin to understand them by the hands-on labs. . . . I found that I understand the lessons better when we are able to do hands-on and get to experience and find what it is about ourselves."
>
> *Melissa, end of first nine weeks*
>
> "This school year has been unexplainable. I have improved so much over this past year I don't know where to begin. . . . For once I actually worked hard on my work. Instead of waiting till the last minute to do work, I had to start right when it was given. I learned that the harder you work on an assignment, the more likely you will get a good grade."
>
> *Karina, end of year*

You can also use journals for students to write specific information about their subject area. For example, in math, students might focus on explanations.

> ### Sample Math Journal Prompts
> - Explain a formula.
> - Write about a time that you were really confused in math class. What did you do? Who did you get help from? How did you explain what was confusing you?

- Write about a time that you helped explain something to a classmate. What was your classmate having difficulty with? How did you help your classmate?
- Write everything you know about (choose a math topic).
- Write as many examples as possible of a ratio that you can think of in five minutes.

You could also use a simple two-column chart.

How I solved the problem	*Why I wrote/drew each step*

In science classes, students could keep a fieldbook as they work through the scientific process.

Sample Questions for Science Fieldbook
- What did you observe?
- What did it sound like, look like, or feel like?
- What do you think might occur or what is your hypothesis?
- What variables (or things) might impact the results?
- What will you do next?

Other ways for students to continually process their learning is through blog entries or Twitter chats. Both utilize technology to maximize student motivation in the learning process.

Special Strategy: Using Post-It Notes

The final strategy I'd like to share combines using writing to process learning with demonstrating learning. It's an excellent writing activity that balances individual work with collaborative work. Let's look at a general way to use the activity then an alternate.

Choose pictures from magazines or newspapers (you can use a variety or center all your pictures around a theme or topic). Paste the pictures on the front of a folder. Have students in small groups (four or five maximum) look at the picture and individually write words that describe the picture on small post-it notes (one word per note). Use a time limit of 2–3 minutes, depending on your group.

Next, have the group work together to put their words in categories that are similar (you can use nouns/verbs/adjectives or some other way of categorizing words based on the standards and objectives of the lesson).

The group then uses their notes to build a sentence describing the picture. They will need to use additional post-its to add articles and needed punctuation. Ask groups to share their sentences and pictures and lead a short discussion of expressive writing. Next, have the students individually write paragraphs about their picture, using the sentence and notes as a starting point. For students who need additional assistance with writing, they can use the word bank created by their group. Note that you can focus on any topic, whether it is numbers, planets, or characters from a story.

Next, let's adapt the activity for comparison and contrast. Choose pictures from news or magazine stories (be sure to save the accompanying story). Have students in small groups (four or five maximum) look at the picture and individually write words that describe the picture on small post-it notes (one word per note). Use a time limit of 2–3 minutes, depending on your group.

Next, have the group work together to put their words in categories that are similar (you can use nouns/verbs/adjectives or some other way of categorizing words based on the standards and objectives of the lesson).

The group then uses their notes to build a sentence describing the picture. They will need to use additional post-its to add articles and needed punctuation. For a basic sentence-building/vocabulary building activity, you may stop the lesson at this point, or have the students individually write descriptive paragraphs about the picture, using the sentence and notes as a starting point. *Groups can share their work at this point, or later in the lesson.*

Stage Two

Have the students look at the headline of the accompanying story.

Using a K-W-L chart, have each group write what they already THINK they know about the story, using the headline and the picture. Next, have members of the groups read the article. Compare and contrast the accuracy of the original sentence with the actual story—did the sentence written from the picture agree with the story? Did it accurately reflect the story? Did it add additional details, etc. Again, the comparison and contrast can be tailored to meet your specific standards and objectives. You may also adapt the writing assignment to meet the specific writing domain or content area you are teaching.

Although this was done with newspaper articles, it is also effective for use with content area reading (particularly new topics in science and social studies or word problems in math). It can also be applied to different types of literature for language arts classrooms.

I particularly like the benefits the folder and post-its provide for students. First, students are motivated with an interactive activity which is designed so that ALL students can contribute to the end product. Then, for students who are lacking in the area of prior knowledge, the scaffolding provided by the first activity allows them to build a basis for understanding.

Writing to Demonstrate Learning

There are a variety of ways to demonstrate learning through writing.

Balloons

I like to use balloons to allow students to demonstrate their learning. Each student writes a fact that he or she learned during class on one of the balloons. Then, working in small groups, students pass their papers to the next group member, who also writes a fact. This continues around the circle until each balloon is full. Students can discuss the material, using the balloons as a prompt. You can also use this for students to write what they learned during outside reading. To add more depth, they can write their fact in the balloon then write a piece of supporting evidence on the string.

One advantage to this strategy is that students are able to learn from each other. If Haley only learned one thing, she can write it on all balloons. Then, when she received her full set of balloons, she can read what other students learned, which may jog her memory or build new knowledge.

Two-Voice Poems

Poetry allows students to creatively demonstrate their learning. In a workshop for prospective teachers, we completed an activity where they compared two perspectives. After drafting the examples, I asked them to write some sample comments that each person or perspective might say, which is sometimes simpler than analyzing a situation. Then, they turned that into a poem of two voices. They wrote the comments as a back-and-forth conversation, which can serve as a scaffolding activity for higher analysis. Before you decide this is only a language arts activity, look at the examples. First, check out a high school social studies sample.

Magna Carta	*Bill of Rights*
I was written by the most elite and powerful citizens other than the leader. It was the unchecked power of the leader that required me to be drafted.	I was written by an everyday citizen to express the beliefs of some but not all of the people
A leader was forced to sign me.	Everyday citizens freely and enthusiastically signed me.
I limited the power of the leader but only for the elites.	I express that every citizen should have the right to basic human aspirations and legal protections from those in power.
I was a long list of the elite's grievances with the ruler but had nothing to do with the average person.	I am also a long list of grievances against the leader but not of the elite, rich, or powerful, but rather, of the average citizen.

(continued)

(continued)

I say that the ruler had to obey their own laws.	I say that the ruler had no legal authority or power over the everyday person.
I resulted in a more stable type of government generations.	I resulted in a major war that saw the world's most powerful and modern military force face-off against an untrained and poorly equipped group of volunteers.
I was signed on the east side of the Atlantic.	I was signed on the west side of the Atlantic.
You can still see me on display in the country in which I was drafted and signed, but I no longer have a legal standing.	You can see me, too, in my country's capitol. What I declared then is just as relevant today as it was when I was signed roughly 250 years ago.

Elementary Teachers Created a Science Sample:

Liquid	*Solid*
Why do you make things so hard?	I am what I am.
You need to go with the flow, like me.	I have a definite shape.
I can take the shape of anything.	Maybe if we heat things up in here, I can change.
But then, I'd disappear.	

Fibonacci Sequence Poems

I read an article in the *New York Times* about a blogger who encourages the use of the Fibonacci sequence to write six-line poems based on syllables. This is a nice math twist on poetry and a more structured way for students to demonstrate they understand a concept.

> **Fibonacci Sequence Poem About Divisibility**
> 1 Math
> 1 House
> 2 Divide
> 3 Whole numbers
> 5 Remainder zero
> 8 When the last digit is even
> 5 Then divide by 2
> 3 The answer
> 2 Should be
> 1 A
> 1 Whole

Amber, Grade 7

Writing to Apply Learning

Finally, you can use writing to help students apply their learning. With application, you want students to go beyond what they learned to apply it in a new way.

RAFT Strategy

One way for students to apply their learning is the RAFT Strategy. Perhaps you would like your students to write a paragraph about the solar system (the topic you have been teaching in class). This is a standard assignment to demonstrate learning that requires students to restate or summarize the information that you have covered. We can increase the rigor and move to application using the RAFT strategy (Santa, Havens, &

Macumber, 1996). RAFT stands for *role, audience, format,* and *topic*. Using this strategy, students assume a role, such as an astronaut, and write from that perspective to a more authentic audience, such as people who read his online blog. In this case, students are required to understand the topic at a higher level in order to complete the task.

Role	*Audience*	*Format*	*Topic*
Host Ole Winfrey	Television viewing audience	Talk show	Interviewing Aztecs about their culture
Word problem	Student	Directions	How to solve the equation embedded in the problem
Comma	Young authors	Op ed piece	Misuses of the comma
Water drop	New water drops	Travel guide	Water cycle
Musical note	Composer	Persuasive letter	Usefulness in symphony
Computer programmer	Venture capitalist (funding provider)	Design for new video game	Conflict in the Middle Ages

Profiles

Another way to apply learning is through creating profiles of main characters, historical figures, famous people, or job descriptions. For example, in a social studies classroom, students can create video blogs of a person from history. In order to do so, they must apply what they have learned about the person to create personal accounts for the video blogs.Similarly, students could research a scientist and create a fake Facebook page.

Chad Maguire, a math teacher, asks his students to research and write about a famous mathematician. After giving students an overview of the project and sharing brief biographies of mathematicians, he randomly draws students' names, and they hold a draft similar to a professional sports draft to select their subjects. The finished report must include standard information about the person, but students also present the information in a creative way, such as role-playing the mathematician or creating a game. As a final incentive, students earn additional points based on the number of things they have in common with the person they research. The last part of the project requires students to move beyond basic information to application to their own lives.

Follow the Yellow Brick Road

Another creative strategy for applying knowledge is "Follow the Yellow Brick Road." Place bricks on the floor to create a road—one that divides into three paths. Students write notes with applications to other topics in your class, other classes, or their own lives.

Gallery Walk

A final strategy is to adapt the "Gallery Walk" we discussed earlier. Students do gallery walks to look at finished products, usually a project. In this case, you create the items to post around the room. Students visit each product, which can be as simple as a paragraph of information, or more complex, such as a series of tweets, a Facebook page, or a mockup of a webpage, and they identify the mistake in each one. Requiring students to assess information and identify misconceptions is a much more rigorous skill. Using a sample grid, students note the incorrect information.

Gallery Walk Grid	
Station	Misconceptions or Mistakes
1—Title	
2—Title	
3—Title	
4—Title	
5—Title	

Key Ideas

- Modeling writing is important for students.
- Writing can help students activate their learning.
- Writing is also an effective way for students to process their learning.
- Using writing to demonstrate and apply learning helps students extend what they know.

Thoughts to Consider

1. What are two or three main points you learned?
2. What is one strategy you would like to implement?
3. What is a question you would like to explore in more depth?

7

Formative Assessment Supports Scaffolding

Although formative assessment is important for all students, it is absolutely critical for your struggling learners. Formative assessment, when used correctly, allows you to identify specific weaknesses for struggling students, and then gives you information on their progress. That's how you know what, how, and when to scaffold with your students. As you review the assessment strategies in this chapter, keep in mind the purpose is effective scaffolding. I prefer to use a teach-assess then what flowchart. Teach-Assess Then What?

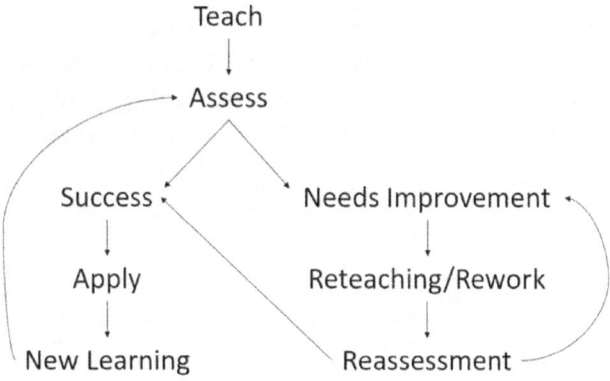

Using that as an overall framework, let's look at three key areas.

> Principles of Effective Assessment
> Goal-Setting for Assessment
> Sample Formative Assessments

Principles of Formative Assessments

There are three principles to remember as you develop and use formative assessments. First, be sure your tool allows students to focus of specific skills you want to assess. For example, if you want to know what students generally understand, an exit slip may work. However, if you want to know if specific content has been mastered, you may want to use an anticipation guide.

Second, provide an opportunity for students to be successful. In other words, find a way for all students to believe they can respond. I found that asking my students to pull out a sheet of paper and write information was too overwhelming for them. They felt like they had to fill up the page, so some didn't write anything. You'll find lots of ways to chunk the assessments in the upcoming pages.

Third, work with students to see progress and set goals.

Right now, I know . . .	
I'm learning . . .	
This is how I plan to get there . . .	

Students need to set and achieve goals to build a sense of confidence, which leads to a willingness to try something else, which, in turn, begins a cycle that leads to higher levels of success. Success leads to success, and the achievements of small goals are building blocks to larger goals.

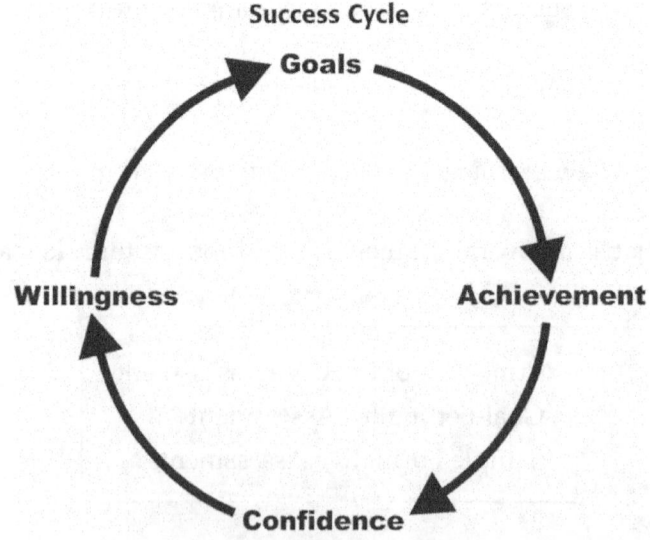

134 ◆ Scaffolding for Success

Student Goal-Setting Activities for Assessment

A good place to start is to talk about goals with students. You can share one of your goals and discuss their goals. You may have to start broader with dreams and then focus on the specific goals. I visited a classroom that had a large bulletin board titled Our Goals. Each student wrote his or her goal and posted it for everyone to see. Many wrote the standard "make good grades," but some wrote more personal ones. Other options are to have students write about their goals in journals. The point is to have them identify their own goals and for you to know about them so you can tie learning to their goals.

I used two different goal-setting activities when I was teaching. First, each of my students created a "Me Poster" at the start of the year. I adapted this idea from one my dad used with teachers during workshops. I provided some starting points using basic pictures or shapes (see Components of Me Poster), and they could customize the posters. This gave me a tremendous amount of information about who they were and their interests and goals—probably more than I would have known if I had merely talked with them or even asked them to write about themselves because many were reluctant writers.

My students and I also enjoyed creating time capsules for each person using paper towel cardboard rolls. At the start of the school year, I asked them to focus on where they were in terms of academics, accomplishments, or interests. Students selected objects that represented different things about themselves, and they put those objects in the tube along with an essay they wrote. They told about themselves using the contents then filled the tube and decorated it. I hung the tubes in the classroom, and at the end of the year, my students opened them and wrote a new essay about how they had changed over the year. Many of them were surprised at how much they had learned and grown.

Components of Me Poster

Star: In what way do you star as a student?
Trading Stamp: What part of your personality would you like to trade in?
Flower Pot: How can you make our classroom a better place to be?
First Prize Ribbon: For what one thing would you like to be remembered?
Crown: What is your crowning achievement?
Winner Sign: Why are you a winner?
Turkey: What are the turkeys that get you down?
Question Mark: What one thing do you want others to know about you?

For shorter-term goals, I like to use file folders and post-it notes. Students decorate a file folder. Then, they can write their goals and post them on the left inside of the folder, and as they master the goals, they can move them to the right side. You can reuse these for any period of time.

Sample Formative Assessments

Let's look at a range of formative assessments that are useful in a classroom.

Stimulate Students' Self-Awareness

In these exit slips, students judge how well they understand the content. For example, you might ask students to rank themselves on a scale of 1–4: 4—I can teach this to another student; 3—I feel comfortable working on my own but may need to use another resource to help me; 2—I understand somewhat but need a different explanation; 1—clueless. Ask students, "How would you rate your understanding of what we discussed in class today?" You might place a laminated poster by your door. On the poster, use a picture of a stoplight, mountain, or another symbol that is relevant to students. Then pose the question. For example, "How comfortable do you feel with using semicolons, colons and dashes in your writing?" Or "How confident are you in your ability to explain the difference between free enterprise and command economy to another student?" Have students write their name on a sticky note and place it on or near the term or picture that matches their comfort level. If you would like students' responses to be confidential, have them write their choice on a notecard and place it in a box near the door.

General Self-Assessment			
On the Road	*Cereals*	*Stoplight*	*Airplane*
I'm stuck in a hole. Help! I may have taken the wrong turn. Can I get some directions?	Frosted Flakes—My brain feels frosted and I don't know what to do.	Red (I'm stuck where I am)	Gate—ready to learn) Yellow (Moved to the runway—getting started)

(continued)

(continued)

I've arrived. I am really comfortable and feel we can move on.	Froot Loops—I feel like I'm stuck in a loop and need some help. Cheerios—I'm cheering because I understand!!	Yellow (I need some help before I move on) Green (Ready to move on)	Purple (At the Green (In the air—everything is fine—I'm where I need to be) Blue (Soaring—moving beyond to new levels)

Subject-Specific Self-Assessment			
Scientist	Mathematician	Author	Historian
Taking a guess- I have a hypothesis, but I haven't determined the steps for an investigation. *Making a plan-* I have outlined my procedures and determined my variables but haven't collected or analyzed data. *Experiment concluded-* I have completed an experiment and either conformed or disproved my hypothesis.	*Laying the foundation-* I've read the problem, but I'm not sure where to start. *Halfway there-* I have determined the procedure needed to solve this problem, but I need help with the numerical computation. *Success achieved-* I have successfully set up the procedure and arrived at an answer through computation.	*Drafting my plan-* just getting started and need help. *Finished with draft-* getting there but I have a few questions. *Ready to publish-* I'm done and ready to move on!	I recognize a conflict that occurred in history, but I'm not sure why it happened or how it was resolved. *Uncovering the past-* I have researched the conflict and understand the who, what, when, where, and why. I still haven't determined how the conflict influenced future generations or established how it's connected to similar conflicts of the time period. *History buff-* I understand the societal/economic/ political impact of this conflict and how it influenced future events and decisions.

Another option is to use *A Bump in the Road*. With a bump in the road, students reflect on their learning and identify two to four points where they hit bumps in the road, or struggles. Then, they partner with another student to see if they can work their way through their struggle.

Checklists

An important formative assessment tool for teachers is the use of checklists. Checklists, which provide a quick way for you to make notes about your observations, can be simple yes/no tallies or they can be open-ended for teachers to add notes. You can use checklists to observe students during videos, monitor chats or other group work, or review tasks or assignments.

Sample Mathematics Checklist	
Characteristic	*Notes*
Student demonstrates problem-solving ability.	
Student demonstrates persistence while solving problems.	
Student reflects on his/her thinking.	
Student shows applications of learning to real-life.	

Sample Language-Arts Checklist	
Characteristic	*Notes*
Student demonstrates ability to write a narrative paragraph.	
Student demonstrates persistence while writing.	

(continued)

(continued)

Sample Language-Arts Checklist	
Characteristic	*Notes*
Student reflects on his/her writing and makes revisions throughout the process.	
Student shows applications of simple conventions (capital letters, punctuation).	

Sample Middle-School Science Checklist	
Characteristic	*Notes*
Student demonstrates an ability to write a hypothesis.	
Student understands controlled and uncontrolled variables in an experiment.	
Student can set up procedures for an experiment.	
Student demonstrates ability to draw conclusions based on data.	

Sample Elementary Social-Studies Checklist	
Characteristic	*Notes*
Student understands the concept of community.	

(*continued*)

(continued)

Sample Elementary Social-Studies Checklist	
Characteristic	*Notes*
Student can identify various roles of members in a community.	
Student can verbalize the rights and responsibilities of citizens in a community and his/her role in the community.	
Student demonstrates awareness of cultural differences and appreciates diversity within his/her community.	

Connections

When teaching new content, consider pausing and asking students to create connections between the new materials and something with which they are familiar. While very difficult for the students because of its abstract nature, it will provide insight into how closely your students are conceptualizing the new material and allow for real-life applications.

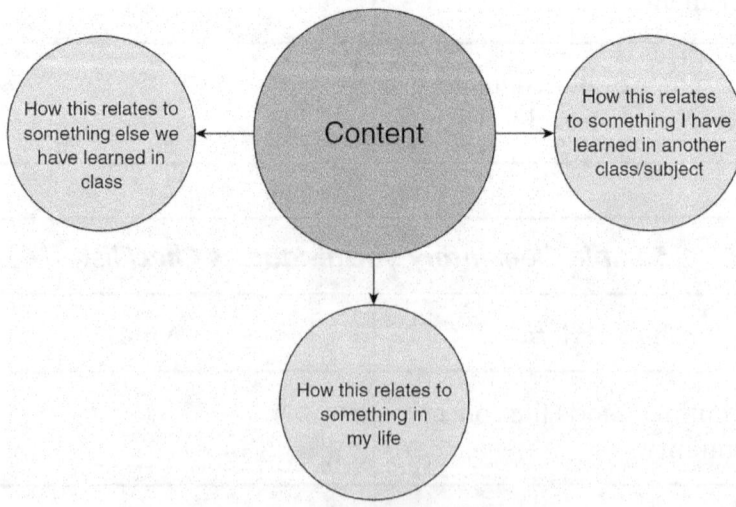

Time to Act

Many students like the notion of acting, being a star, or being a TikTok Influencer. Ask them to prepare 1 minute sharing what they know either by acting in front of the group or creating a video.

Four Corners

You can also use physical "rooms," such as the four corners of your classroom, or chat rooms, Flipdgrids, or YoTeach, which provide for a technological version of four corners. You may ask students to go to Corner A or Chat Room 1 if they strongly support the actions of Stanley Yelnats in *Holes*, Corner B or Chat Room 2 if they agree, Corner C or Chat Room 3 if they disagree, or Corner D or Chat Room 4 if they strongly disagree. They must have a rationale for their decision based on textual evidence. Similarly, you could use Four Corners to review information. After teaching about Ancient Egypt, you could assign students at random to one of four corners to collaborate with new group members: Corner or Chat Room 1—religion/gods; Corner or Chat Room 2—Pharoahs and mummies; Corner or Chat Room 3—architecture/pyramids; Corner or Chat Room 4—government/social classes. These groups return to the general chat to share out, at which point you can address any major points that have been missed and correct any misunderstandings. This is also an excellent option for allowing students to create multiple-choice questions for other groups.

> ### *Tech Connection*
> This is also a good opportunity to mention live virtual breakout chat rooms, such as those incorporated in Zoom. While beneficial, they are difficult to monitor simultaneously. Many school or district policies require continual monitoring. Check with your school or district to see if breakout chat rooms are an option.

Bounce the Ball

In Bounce the Ball, use a beach ball to assess what students know. The first student makes a point about the lesson. Then, they throw the ball to another student, who either expands on the first point, asks a question, or makes another point. The game continues until students run out of points.

Always-Sometimes-Never True

In Always-Sometimes-Never True, the teacher makes a statement that could meet any of the three options. Then, students move to the front, middle, or back of the room to discuss their choice. Finally, the teacher leads a whole-group discussion. This is particularly helpful when there is not a yes or no choice.

Point-Question-Surprise

In *Point-Question-Surprise*, ask students to draw a triangle. In the middle, write the subject you are reviewing. Then, on the right side, ask them to write a point they learned. On the left side, write a question they have. And on the base, write a surprise from the lesson.

ABC-123

Use the alphabet and/or numbers for students to review information. You might post the letters of the alphabet around the room and ask students to write something they know on each letter. If it's more appropriate, such as in a math class, write a series of numbers on the charts. You could also mix the two.

Pizza Wheel

I also like to use a "pizza wheel" to review material that students are assigned to read before class. Rather than simply listing information, using the wheel allows students to visually organize their thinking. Each student writes a fact that he or she learned on one of the pizza slices. Then, working in small groups, students pass their papers to the next group member, who also writes a fact. This continues around the circle until each pizza is full. Students can discuss the material, using the pizza wheels as a prompt.

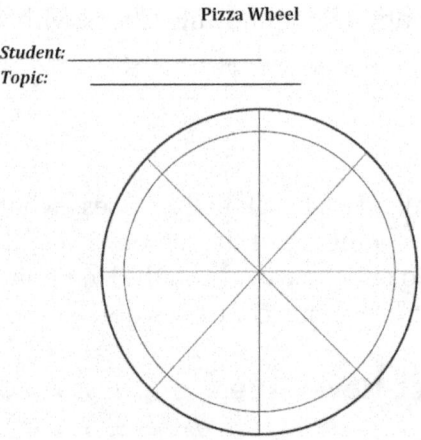

Pizza Wheel

Copyright material from Barbara R. Blackburn (2025), *Scaffolding for Success: Helping Learners Meet Rigorous Expectations Across the Curriculum*, Routledge

Although you can measure your students' understanding in an oral discussion, asking each student to write his or her response ensures that all students are involved in the lesson and provides an opportunity for every student to respond. The rigor is increased, as each student is required to participate.

Sketch It Out/Describe It

Many students enjoy using pictures to demonstrate their learning. In some cases, they will actually demonstrate learning at a higher level than if they write their answers, and for primary students, it is more appropriate. In Sketch It Out, students draw their responses to a prompt. Apps such as You Doodle and Kids Doodle provide students a technology-based option for this activity.

The Most Important Thing

Next, the activity *The Most Important Thing* requires students to prioritize information, identifying the most important learning concept. You can begin by listing information on a chart and having students work together to choose the most important. Over time, they can generate rank items from most to least important.

Exit Slips

One of the most common formative assessment strategies to use after a lesson is an exit slip. However, did you know there are different types of exit slips? It's important to choose the type based on what you want to learn. Also, you may want to mix and match questions for varying types.

> **Types of Exit Slips**
> Demonstrating Understanding of Content
> Reflecting on How They Processed Learning
> Asking Questions
> Self-Assessing Understanding

No matter what type of exit slip you are using, you'll want to find a way to manage the information. With today's technology, there is a variety of ways to collect exit slip information from your students. With any mobile device, students can access a digital platform and immediately push answers out to the teacher, who then has the ability to display the class's thinking as a whole on the screen or choose a select few to further discuss.

Tech Connection
Electronic Exit Slips
- Google Forms
- Mentimeter
- Recap
- Plickers
- Geddit
- Poll Everywhere
- ExitTicket
- Lino
- Padlet (will soon require a fee)

Other Tools

There are many other technology tools that allow you to incorporate formative assessment in your classroom. Let's look at a sampling.

Tech Connection

Formative Assessment Tools	
Online Platform	Functions
Padlet	◆ Acts as digital KWL that can be used to gather student feedback.
Socrative	◆ Develop quizzes, exit tickets, use before or after instruction and organizes data for teacher analysis.
Backchannelchat.com	◆ Pause during a lesson or reading of a text and ask everyone to comment/respond to a question or prompt

(continued)

(continued)

Formative Assessment Tools	
Online Platform	*Functions*
Nearpod.com	♦ Push content out to student devices, one screen at a time, and allow them to interact digitally through multiple choice, open-ended response, annotating text online, drawing on a blank canvas, explore a virtual 3D image, etc. Provides a way for teachers to facilitate a lesson and get immediate realtime feedback as to what your students are thinking.
EdPuzzle	♦ Use any video from a myriad of online sources and insert pause points where students must gather thoughts, answer a question, make a prediction, etc. before they can continue the video. Completely customize a student-directed video lesson and gather feedback via student responses in real time.
Explaineverything.com	♦ Watch your students' thinking. Explain Everything is an interactive whiteboard that asks students to explain their thinking through a problem or through a prompt. Focus on quality over quantity.
Flipgrid	♦ Use any IOS device to create a video response to a question or prompt. Because you can't have a high-quality conversation with every student every day, this allows you to see what they know via explanation.
Kahoot	♦ Use gaming to review! This assessment platform is game based but allows teachers to create content and disaggregate data.

(*continued*)

(continued)

Formative Assessment Tools	
Online Platform	*Functions*
Go Formative	♦ Upload documents, create your own questions, embed videos or pictures . . . and receive immediate data on student performance.

Key Ideas

- Understanding the principles of effective formative assessment will help you plan.
- Goal-setting helps students develop ownership of their assessments.
- Using a variety of formative assessments will help you know how to best target your scaffolding.

Thoughts to Consider

1. What are two or three main points you learned?
2. What is one strategy you would like to implement?
3. What is a question you would like to explore in more depth?

8
Social and Emotional Skills for Scaffolding

In recent years, there has been a focus on Social and Emotional Learning, which includes the areas of self-awareness, self-management, social awareness, relationship skills, and responsible decision-making.

In this chapter, we're going to focus on seven specific social and emotional skills that can support struggling students. They are part of an overall strategy for scaffolding learning.

> Growth Mindset
> Goal-Setting
> Relationship Building
> Decision-Making and Problem-Solving
> Confidence
> Organizational skills

Growth Mindset

As Carol Dweck explains, a fixed mindset assumes that our character, intelligence, and creative ability are static and cannot be changed. A growth mindset, on the other hand, adopts the perspective that our intelligence, creativity, and character can change and grow over time.

These two views have a tremendous impact on teaching and learning. If a teacher believes in a fixed mindset, then he or she is saying there is no potential for growth. If a child is intelligent, they will continue to be so. If a child is struggling, it's because he or she just isn't "smart enough." On the other hand, if you believe in a growth mindset, you believe that students may start with a certain amount of ability, but that can change over time with effort and persistence.

For students, which of these they believe also matters. Students with a fixed mindset typically avoid challenges, feel threatened by others' successes, and give up easily. They want to look smart and believe that working hard at a task means they are not smart.

Students with a growth mindset believe they can learn and become better. They embrace challenge, view effort as a positive part of learning, and persist through difficulties. Nigel Holmes provides a clear breakdown of the two mindsets discovered by Dr. Dweck. As you read the chart, see if you can identify these traits in your struggling learners.

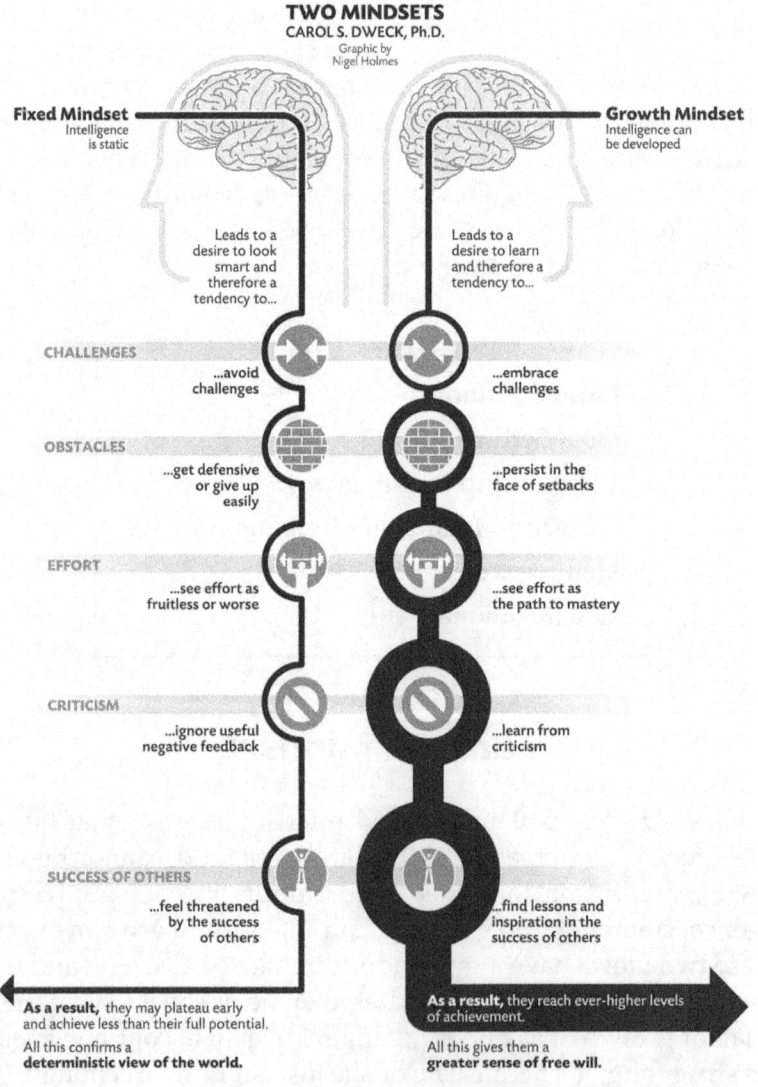

By Professor Carol Dweck, graphic by Nigel Holmes. Used with permission from Nigel Holmes.

Build a Learning-Oriented Mindset

First, we need to ensure that students have a learning-oriented mindset. Often, they don't. Most of my struggling learners had given up, believing they could never learn. I'll never forget Erika, who said, "Why are you bothering? Don't you know I'm stupid?"

We start the process by having this mindset ourselves then constantly and consistently reinforcing it with students. We do this by providing the right support for them to learn, encouraging them along the path, and celebrating their resilience and success.

Teachers can also ensure that all students are engaged in the learning process. Although we have looked at strategies to engage struggling students throughout this book, here, I want to share a specific questioning technique that is particularly effective for struggling learners. In *Engaging Students with Poverty in Mind*, Erik Jensen (2013) describes the difference between exclusive and inclusive questions. Particularly when we are activating prior knowledge, we ask questions to elicit students' experiences. However, at times, our questions may exclude struggling students, since they may not have a wide base of experiences.

Instead, use questions that are more inclusive. Take a look at the samples below.

Exclusive vs. Inclusive Questions	
Exclusive	*Inclusive*
Who has ever traveled out of our city?	Who would like to travel somewhere different?
Who read a book outside of school lately?	I just read a book about xxx. Have you ever heard, read, or seen a movie about that?
Who completed their homework last night?	How many of you remember that we had homework last night? Can anyone tell me what it was about?
Raise your hand if you have been to an art museum.	Raise your hand if you've ever seen a picture you liked.

Source: Adapted from Jensen (2013) *Engaging Students with Poverty in Mind*

Using inclusive questions will help you engage your struggling students at a higher level as well as help them see they can contribute to the discussion.

Reinforce Effort

Encouraging and reinforcing effort are particularly critical for those students who do not understand the importance of their own efforts. In *Classroom Instruction that Works*, Marzano, Pickering, and Pollock (2001) make two important comments regarding students' views about effort.

Research-Based Generalizations About Effort
- Not all students realize the importance of believing in effort.
- Students can learn to change their beliefs to an emphasis on effort.

(Marzano, Pickering, & Pollock, 2001, p. 50)

This is positive news for teachers. First, we're not imagining it—students don't realize they need to exert effort. And second, we can help them change that belief. Richard Curwin describes seven specific ways to encourage effort.

Seven Ways to Encourage Effort
1. Never fail a student who tries, and never give the highest grades to one who doesn't.
2. Start with the positive.
3. See mistakes as learning opportunities, not failures.
4. Give do-overs.
5. Give students the test before you start a unit.
6. Limit your corrections.
7. Do not compare students.

Goal-Setting

Goal-setting is both a way to empower students (when we set goals for them) and for them to demonstrate ownership (when they set and track their own goals). There are five aspects to effective goals.

> **Effective Goals**
> Growth-Driven
> Offer Structure
> Attainable
> Learning-Oriented
> Specific

Growth-Driven

First, effective goals are growth-driven. In other words, they are focused on progress. For example, a growth-driven goal for a secondary student struggling with study skills might be: *To increase my understanding of content, demonstrated by a higher grade on my report card, by taking notes in class, annotating the notes, and reviewing them daily*. Although there are specific steps to achieve the goal that are include, notice there is an emphasis on increasing understanding. Students need to see that progress is what is important, in addition to achieving certain benchmarks.

Offer Structure

Goals should also offer structure to students. Notice, in the prior goal, that the increased understanding will come from taking notes in class, annotating the notes, and reviewing them daily. Those are three detailed actions that are shown to increase comprehension. The structure also includes a time frame—these are actions to take daily. Finally, there is a guideline for success—demonstrated by a higher grade on the report card.

Attainable

Goals should also be attainable. One of my students wanted to set a goal that he would earn an A in all his classes. Prior to this, he had a D average. Although I wanted to have high expectations, I didn't want to set him up for failure. We agreed that the focus would be to improve his grade at least one letter grade in reading/language arts and in math and that we would make similar goals for the other subjects during the next grading period. He reluctantly agreed, and he agreed to concentrate additional effort in those two subjects. We also discussed exactly what he needed to do to achieve a higher grade, and I built in additional support (including learning packets he could work on at home) for him. The result? At the end of the grading period, he earned a B in Math and a C in Reading/Language Arts. He was very proud, and his confidence soared. Over the year, he continued to work in all subjects and ended the year with a B average.

Learning-Oriented

Larry Ferlazzo, in *Self-Driven Learning* (2013), points out there are two types of goals. Sometimes we set performance goals, such as "I'll make an A"; alternatively, we set learning goals like "I'll read more challenging books." Although both are acceptable, learning goals provide more authenticity for students. Performance goals can actually narrow a student's focus and can impede progress when there is not a direct relationship between the goal and the outcome. For example, if my goal is to make an A and I study hard and only make a B, it can undermine my self-confidence.

Learning goals are far more effective. They provide opportunities for students to find creative ways to meet their goals, use problem-solving strategies, and focus on overall improvement rather than a single point in time.

Specific

Finally, goals must be specific. Sometimes, in our zeal to write goals that are attainable, we make them too broad. For example, *I will do better in class* may be a worthy goal, but how is it measured? What does it mean? Better in terms of behavior? Grades? We need to go back to some of our earlier examples and reframe it as: *During the next two weeks, I will improve my behavior by staying in my seat and not interrupting my teacher when she is talking. I will improve my learning by completing my work on time, asking my teacher for help when I need it, finishing my homework, and staying after school for help on Thursdays.*

Goal-Setting Activities

I like using vision letters, folders, and posters to help struggling students describe their goals. In a vision letter, students imagine it is the end of the school year (or grading period) and that, as they look backward, they discover being in x grade was their best year ever. They write a letter to a friend describing what made being in that grade so great, and by doing so, they define their vision for a good year.

In this sample, a ninth grader wrote her letter for the second semester in Algebra 1. Shakierra was a student who struggled in math first semester, but you can tell from the letter she wanted to improve.

> Dear Ms. Ray,
>
> My second semester was the most successful because my mind was focused on school instead of everything else. Especially in Algebra 1 because this is a class we have to really be focused in to pass. Instead of speeding through my work like usual I took my time and reviewed my work after completing it. Even though I still had some of my mind on boys I still stayed focused on my work too.
>
> My second semester was also successful because I let my sister help me and teach me new ways instead of arguing with her and telling her I knew what I am doing when I didn't know. I watched my cousin teach his brother different ways to do Algebra. That's why my second semester was successful.
>
> Shakierra

After reading the letter, the teacher met with Shakierra. They agreed to take several steps to help Shakierra improve. The teacher moved Shakierra to the front of the room to help her avoid looking at boys in class. Shakierra agreed to have her sister or cousin sign off on her homework. By the end of the semester, Shakierra earned a B in class.

You can adapt this with folders and posters. In these cases, students cut out or draw pictures or words and paste them on the poster to showcase their vision. If you choose to use a folder, you can use the panels to divide the year into four time periods, setting a vision for smaller intervals.

Another goal-setting activity is to use the Pizza Wheel (see Chapter 7). Students write different categories around the wheel such as homework, reading, math, friends, etc., then write their goals for each area. You can revisit the goals periodically.

Relationship Building

Relationship building is another critical social skill. Tom Roderick, Executive Director of Morningside Center for Teaching Social Responsibility and author of *A School of Our Own: Parents, Power, and Community at the*

East Harlem Block Schools, describes several community-building activities to foster a culture of respect.

Sample SEL Activities

Name Games are a good way to start off the year. Kids stand in a circle and toss a soft ball to each other. When a student catches the ball, the class shouts out the student's name. The game continues till everyone gets a shout-out.

Have a Heart dramatizes the importance of making the classroom a "put-down-free zone." With a construction paper heart taped to her chest, the teacher tells the story of a student who experiences put-downs throughout her day. At each put-down, the teacher tears a piece from the heart. After a brief discussion ("Have you ever had a day like this? How do put-downs make us feel?"), she retells the story. But this time, the class substitutes put-ups for the put-downs.

Think Differently encourages students of all ages to engage in lively debate while acknowledging that we can disagree—and still treat each other with respect. The teacher tapes a "Strongly Agree" sign on one side of the classroom and a "Strongly Disagree" sign on the other. The teacher makes a statement, and students move to one sign or the other depending on whether they agree or disagree. If they're undecided, they stand in the middle. Statements can range from the trivial ("Vanilla ice cream is best") to the more serious ("Kids should only be allowed to watch one hour of TV per day" or "Slavery was the cause of the Civil War"). The teacher asks students in each group to explain their view, and students change position if they change their mind during the discussion. If the debate gets too heated, the teacher can ask students to paraphrase the opinion just expressed before putting out their own.

Source: http://novofoundation.org/newsfromthefield/several-ways-to-apply-social-emotional-learning-strategies-in-the-classroom/

Another way to help students build relationships is through specified roles and responsibilities. Tamara Willis, seventh-grade social studies teacher at Sullivan Middle School, chose a this approach after her students complained, "School is like a job and . . . we should get paid for attending." Her students voted to create a business, which was named Sullivan University. Students prepared resumes and applied for positions (Dean, Professor, and Intern) and interviewed one another for the jobs. Those students who were hired to be deans held an executive board meeting with Ms. Willis to form teams and design new classroom rules to address issues related to poor behavior and absenteeism.

As the experiment continued, students began to demonstrate leadership by quieting their peers when they were disruptive. The result? Attendance increased, students were more engaged in instruction, and discipline referrals decreased.

Amber Chandler, author of *The Flexible SEL Classroom*, provides a template that can be used with projects. Students apply to complete a project, specifying what they will do, how they will do it, and how they will present it. They must also describe how they will use their time and who will assume each rule. By doing so, they learn to work together in a group.

Names of proposed members (not to exceed 5):

_____	email: _____
_____	email: _____
_____	email: _____
_____	email: _____
_____	email: _____

Brief description of the process, product, and presentation you are planning:
Process: (What will the group be doing or exploring? What is your burning question?)
_____
_____

Product: (What will you be making or creating to "show what you know"?)
_____
_____

Presentation: (How will you share what you have learned? Who is the authentic audience? What technology will you use?)
_____
_____

Planning your time:
For each project we do, there is a presentation to prepare and a written component, so the work must be done by everyone involved. Please sign up for the role(s) that you will commit to. This means that you will create the slides and the written part of the document. Read the expectations carefully, as there are different amounts of work.

When, outside of class, do you have to work on this together? This could be studyhalls, Facetiming, in my room either before or after school, or via Google Classroom.
_____
_____

You need to be aware that your grades will be calculated this way:
The products from your role + group essay grade = Avg of the two → essay grade (test)
Group slideshow grade + your job presenting = presentation grade (test)

In the group, you need to decide on the following (some may have to do more than one position):
_____ Researcher
_____ Lead Writer
_____ Time Manager
_____ Tech Coordinator
_____ Lead Presenter
_____ Editor
_____ Project Manager

*By signing this agreement, you recognize that this is a huge project with three major test grades associated with it, as well as many classwork grades. You realize that when you submit slides or essays that you are ALL responsible for the spelling, mechanics, and grammar, as well as if it makes sense. You don't have to edit content, but the document and slides must be correct. There will be one slideshow submitted and one essay. All names must be clearly stated. If you become a burden to your group by not doing work on the planned timeline, you may be removed to complete the project yourself.

_____   _____
Student   date

_____   _____
Student   date

_____   _____
Student   date

_____   _____
Student   date

_____   _____
Student   date

Decision-Making and Problem-Solving

Decision Charts are away for students to view an issue from a variety of perspectives and finalize a decision. Following the template below, students write the issue. Next, they write the different options that could occur in response to the issue. Finally, they write the pros and cons of each response. The charts can then be used as a starting point for a class or small group discussion, an essay or extended response, or a debate.

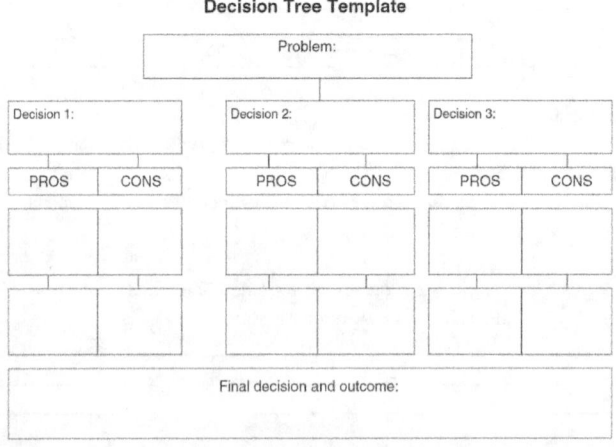

Copyright material from Barbara R. Blackburn (2025), *Scaffolding for Success: Helping Learners Meet Rigorous Expectations Across the Curriculum*, Routledge

Problem-Solving

Cubing allows students to look at a topic or issue from six perspectives in order to solve a problem. At a basic level, the sides of the cube are labeled who, what, when, where, why, and how. Students would then write about or answer the questions for each side of the block. You can use cubing to ask students to solve problems such as "who is the hero," "who is the villain," "what is the best solution," or "which choice should I make."

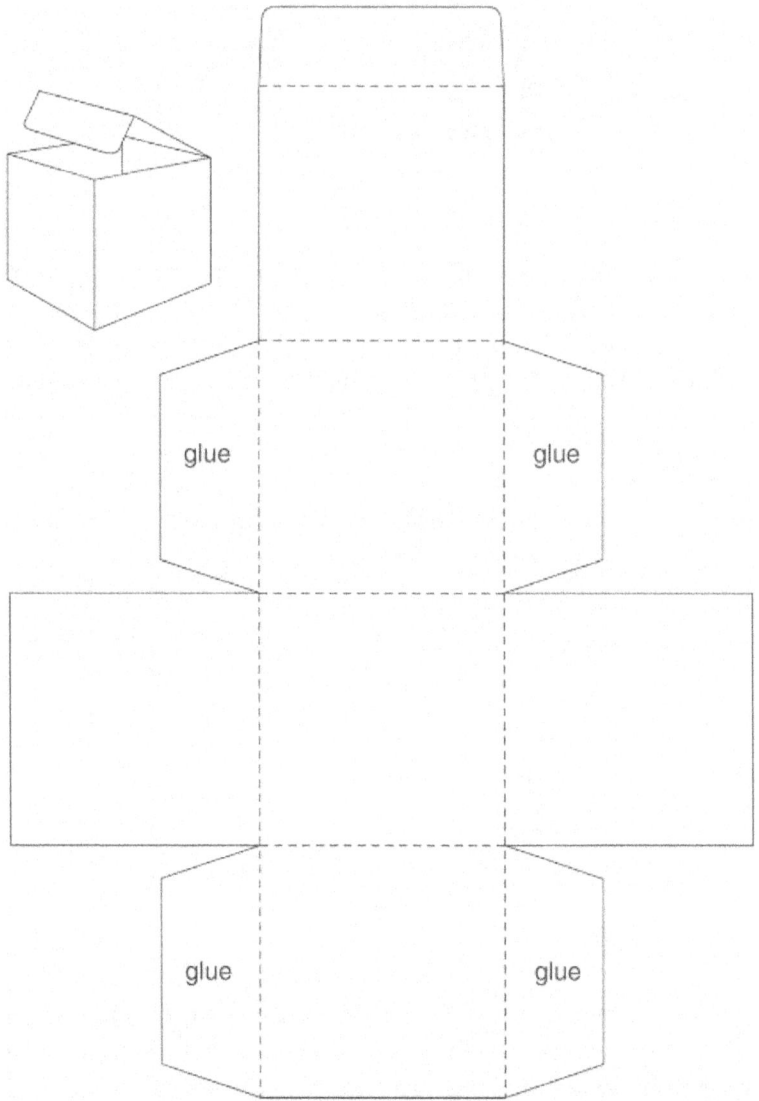

Copyright material from Barbara R. Blackburn (2025), *Scaffolding for Success: Helping Learners Meet Rigorous Expectations Across the Curriculum*, Routledge

When I was teaching, I used more sophisticated prompts for writing, such as analysis and application. They required my students to move beyond a basic answer to more complex responses.

> **Cubing Prompts**
> Describe it (the topic or issue)
> Compare it
> Associate it
> Analyze it
> Apply it
> Argue for or against it

One of the benefits of cubing is that you can use a variety of prompts, depending on your specific grade level and/or subject area. A caution, however: Be sure your prompts are appropriate for the topic and encourage higher level thinking, rather than just being a cute worksheet.

> **Other Possible Cubing Prompts**
> Define it
> Explain it
> Locate it
> Solve it
> Illustrate it
> Diagram it
> Research it
> Write a sentence (or paragraph) with it

A final way to use cubes is to write different assignments on each side of the cube. Students can "roll the cube" physically or electronically (random.org) to determine their activity or you can assign specific sides to them. It's a great option for differentiating instruction.

Confidence

Many of our struggling students lack confidence. They don't believe they can be successful, especially in school. One of the first things you can do is to encourage your struggling learners. Many authors distinguish between praise and encouragement. Lavoie (2007) points out that praise is conditional; you receive it when you have done something. Encouragement, on the other hand, is unconditional and can be used even when a student is unsuccessful. It is not judgmental.

Years ago, I saw a cartoon that exemplified the difference between praise and encouragement. It showed a cartoon character fishing. In the first frame, the character caught a huge fish and others were congratulating him. That's praise. In the second frame, he caught a shoe. None of the bystanders spoke to him except one little boy, who said, "You did catch something. That's better than nothing. Are you going to try again?" That's encouragement.

Encouragement supports students and focuses on progress. You can do this through praise, but there is a different emphasis with encouragement. Rather than comparing a student to others or a set standard, encouragement values the student, not the performance.

Next, you can provide activities that will build confidence in your students. I asked my students to do a timeline of their achievements. They could put anything they were proud of on their timelines, both in and outside of school. We also provided space to add items throughout the year.

Another way to build confidence is with 3 Good Points. At the end of every day, students write "3 Good Points" in a journal or planner. It can be something good that happened to them, an accomplishment, or a way they helped someone. By journaling them, they can reflect back when they are struggling to remember they can be successful.

A final way to build confidence is to help students reframe their internal conversations from negative to positive. You may have to model this multiple times, as well as post sample positive comments to help students.

Sample Negative Comments	*Sample Positive Comments*
I can't believe I did that!	Can I build on what I've done?
Am I really that stupid?	I know I can do it.
I'll never accomplish anything.	I can accomplish anything if I work hard.

Organizational Skills

Organization

Our final skill is organization. For this, I turned to my good friend, Dr. Frank Buck, a Top 10 Global Guru in Time Management and the author of *Get Organized Digitally! The Educator's Guide to Time Management*. Here are his five habits designed to bring the gift of organization to the struggling student.

Write It Down

Provide the student with an agenda book. Those little squares give the student a single place to write down homework assignments. But help the student expand that use. This one book also becomes the place for test dates, athletic practices, club meetings, family activities, music practice, and personal goals. The simple act of writing it down makes forgetting a thing of the past. Let pencil and paper do the remembering and reminding.

Students love their phones. For the older student who has mastered the art of the agenda book, the phone can serve as the digital substitute. A calendar, such as Google Calendar, provides a single place to record everything. The phone meets one basic requirement of a good organizational tool—it's with the student all the time. The practice of putting homework commitments on the digital calendar must be as immediate as it is with the paper agenda book.

Establish an "Office"

School becomes easier when the student has a dedicated place at home. A small desk or even a table is sufficient. Stock the space with paper, a stapler, a tape dispenser, a ruler, pens, pencils, a highlighter, glue, and a pencil sharpener. Everything the student needs is in one place.

Create an "Inbox"

Seamless communication between home and school makes everyone's life easier. When the student has papers for the parents to sign, where does the student put them?

Having an "inbox" removes the guesswork. The student has one spot to put anything for the parents. The grownups have only one place to look. Guess who also needs an "inbox"? The student! Create a single folder. Loose papers from the teacher go there. Loose papers going back to school need to go in this folder. The "inbox" is the place for anything that needs action: a worksheet to complete, an article to read, a permission slip to be signed, or a signed permission slip to return to the teacher. It's the one place for all the "loose ends" come together and those loose ends are resolved.

Conduct "Spring Cleaning"

Even the most organized household needs maintenance. A good "spring cleaning" uncovers items in the wrong place, things to be adjusted, and some other things to be thrown away.

Have the student do a "spring cleaning" periodically. What papers have collected at the bottom of the bookbag? What papers have been folded in half and stuck inside textbooks? Does everything in that notebook still need to be there, or can assignments from months ago now be filed or thrown away?

In our digital world, the same principles apply. Have the student go through those Google Drive folders. Trash files no longer of value. Create folders for older material not needed now but which still serves as good reference information. Whether it's paper or digital, when the clutter is gone, it's easier to find the good stuff.

Begin Tomorrow Today

Forgotten items and frantic mornings lead to a poor start of the school day. Morning is a terrible time to finish that last bit of homework or hunt for a missing shoe.

Get everything ready the night before. Choose tomorrow's outfit. Put everything going to school in the book bag.

When morning comes, there's no confusion about what to wear or what to gather before heading off to school. It's a great start to a great day!

Key Ideas

- Skills related to social and emotional learning support scaffolding.
- Focusing on growth mindset and goal-setting matters to students.

- Helping students build relationships also helps learning.
- Providing opportunities for decision-making and problem-solving builds confidence.
- Teaching students to develop organizational skills builds their opportunities for success.

Thoughts to Consider

1. What are two or three main points you learned?
2. What is one strategy you would like to implement?
3. What is a question you would like to explore in more depth?

9

Common Concerns About Scaffolding

I hear many questions from teachers related to scaffolding, but in this chapter, we'll discuss the four I receive most often.

> How do I motivate students who aren't motivated?
> How do I manage everything on my to-do list?
> What about homework?
> How can I partner effectively with parents of struggling students?

How Do I Motivate Students Who Aren't Motivated?

Many teachers tell me, "My struggling students just aren't motivated." If you've read *Motivating Struggling Learners: 10 Strategies to Build Student Success*, you know that I believe all students are motivated, just not necessarily by the things we would like. Many of our students are not motivated by a desire to learn; rather, they are motivated by the approval of their friends or the wish to earn some money or something else in their lives. To build a rigorous classroom environment, we need to encourage students' intrinsic motivation so they are not totally dependent on outside rewards.

Students are more motivated when they value what they are doing and when they believe they have a chance for success. Those are the two keys: value and success. Do students see value in your lesson? Do they believe they can be successful?

Value

There are many recommendations relating rigor to relevance. That is the value part of motivation. Students are more motivated to learn when they see value or the relevance of learning. Students have a video stream playing in their heads: WII-FM—*What's In It for Me?* When we are teaching, students are processing information through that filter. What's in this lesson for me? Why do I need to learn this? Will I ever use this again?

Ideally, your students will make their own connections about the relevance of content, and you should provide them opportunities to make those connections independently. But there are also times that you will need to facilitate that understanding. There was a first-grade teacher who, at the beginning of the year, asked students what their favorite thing to is. He was beginning a lesson on insects. He asked Shaun why it's important to learn about bugs Shaun said, "I don't know, I hate bugs." The teacher said, "Do you like honey?" Shaun got excited and said, "Yes!" The teacher proceeded with some quick information about importance of bees and bee pollination. Shaun became more motivated to learn because he connected with the importance of a food he liked being sustained.

Real-Life Connections
- Measurement attributes: using height and weight to describe themselves
- Whole numbers: discovering missing amounts such as how much more money needed to buy candy
- Interdependent relationships and ecosystems: how plants grow from seeds to edible food
- Water distribution in the Earth: how much drinkable water do we have available
- Weather: how to dress for current weather

Students can also see value in activities and in their relationship with you. When we can provide a hands-on, interactive learning experience, students are more engaged and motivated. Students also find value in their relationships. For example, if you think about your most motivated students, you likely had a good relationship with them. Conversely, with your least motivated students, there was probably not a positive connection. It takes time to build a good relationship with our students, but it is an important part of our role as a teacher.

> **Ways to Connect With Students**
> - Smile, even if you don't feel like it.
> - Have namecards on desks or tables the first day of school so they know you care they are here.
> - Ask them questions about their interests outside of school.
> - Form positive relationships with parents.
> - Incorporate their interests into lessons.
> - Attend one of their extracurricular events.
> - Incorporate ways to learn about them in your instruction.
> - Communicate routine and instructional procedures to parents often.

Success

Success is the second key to student motivation. Students need to achieve in order to build a sense of confidence, which is the foundation for a willingness to try something else. That, in turn, begins a cycle that results in higher levels of success, both in academic performance and in college and career readiness. Success leads to success, and the achievements of small goals or tasks are building blocks to larger ones. Success has been the focus of this book. Throughout, we've discussed ways to help students succeed.

How Do I Manage Everything on My To-Do List?

Another common concern I hear is how to do everything there is to do to meet the needs of struggling students. I understand it takes more time to provide appropriate scaffolding. And, although I can't give you more time, I can provide some strategies that can help.

> **Strategies for Your Current Situation**
> 1. Accept that you will never have as much time or resources as you would like.
> 2. Accept that the quest for perfectionism may be your enemy.
> 3. Work with other teachers.
> 4. Create a Personal Learning Network.
> 5. Work smarter, not harder.
> 6. Remember that small changes lead to bigger ones.
> 7. Keep balance in your life.

Strategy 1: Accept that you will never have as much time or resources as you would like. I continue to find that, no matter how much I have to do, I always need more time. I told a friend of mine once that I wished I had 48 hours per day. She replied, "If that happened, you would end up with double the work!" I find inspiration from Maya Angelou: *If you don't like something, change it. If you can't change it, change your attitude. Don't complain.*

Strategy 2: Accept that the quest for perfectionism may be your enemy. I have realized that there are times my expectations for myself are too high and are, at times, unrealistic. I've also found that to be true with many teachers. They spend hours on the internet looking for ideas to create the perfect lesson plan when they probably could have accomplished just as much if they had stopped much earlier. I'm not recommending you provide sloppy instruction. What I am saying is that, most of the time, 80% of excellence is still very, very good. If it takes you double or triple the time to gain that additional 20%, it's probably not worth it because of all the other tasks you didn't accomplish.

Strategy 3: Work with other teachers. Although it takes time to meet with other teachers to plan together, in the long run, it saves time. Let's say that you have an upcoming unit in a history class that includes reading a primary source that is likely to be challenging for some students. You need a support tool for struggling students, and that will be needed multiple times during the year. Working with the two other teachers who also teach the same subject and grade level, you divide the work. You write the interactive study guide that some students will need for this unit. Your neighbor writes one for Unit 3, and the teacher down the hall is going on maternity leave but volunteers to create one for Unit 6 when she returns. Yes, it takes time for you to write one, but you end up with three when you share, which saves you time in the long run.

Strategy 4: Create a Personal Learning Network. Sometimes, you and your colleagues will need other ideas. I spoke with a teacher who waited until the last minute to plan lessons then frantically googled for ideas. If you have ever done that, you know that you have to filter through a lot of mediocre ideas before you find ones you like. Instead, consider creating your own Personal Learning Network (PLN). It's a way of using the internet and social media to manage your own learning and to organize the information you receive. PLNs are not new. Often, they are just networks of professional contacts, but with social media, it's possible to add experts and colleagues from around the world to your network.

Sources for Building Your PLNs

Twitter/X (for a list of hashtags and chat schedules see http://cybraryman.com/edhashtags.html)

The Educator's PLN (http://edupln.ning.com)

Facebook Groups

EdWeb (https://home.edweb.net)

Classroom 2.0 (www.classroom20.com)

Four Recommended Groups from the THE Journal (https://thejournal.com/articles/2015/10/06/4-fantastic-and-free-professional-learning-networks-for-teachers.aspx)

Edutopia's PLN (www.edutopia.org/blogs/tag/personal-learning-network)

Strategy 5: Work smarter, not harder. You've probably heard this before, but it is true. Far too often, we spend extra time on our work because we can't find something we need or we don't remember something we wanted to change this year. It is absolutely critical to stay organized so that we streamline what we do. Find or create an organizational system that will help you manage all your tasks. There are technology-based options as well as paper ones. I find it particularly helpful to have strategies to document changes I want to make when I teach a lesson next year, collect resources I want to use, and keep up with recurring tasks, such as a weekly email to parents.

When I was a teacher, I addressed the first option by writing notes on my plans. The problem was that I wasn't organized enough to find all my notes when I needed them. Now, to keep up with resources I want to use in the future, I use folders for organization. I keep paper folders, folders in my email, and bookmark folders for my browser, all of which include resources and information I can use. One tip I've learned is that I need to have specific topics on folders, rather than just a miscellaneous one, which makes it more difficult to find resources.

Examples of Folders

Videos
Sample Lessons
Teaching Tips

> Sites for Virtual Field Trips
>
> Blogs
>
> State Standards and Resources Related to Standards
>
> Specific Topics on a Subject (such as force and motion, properties and change, and conservation and transfer) *Again, it's better to be specific, even if you have more folders.*

In terms of recurring tasks, I currently use a to-do list app that allows me to check a box if it occurs regularly, and it automatically schedules it (for example, on the last day of the month). A friend of mine, Frank Buck, mentioned earlier, provides practical ideas and resources on organization and time management, especially using technology, on his website: www.frankbuck.org.

Strategy 6: Remember that small changes lead to bigger ones. Far too often, we think that, if we are implementing something new, we need to change everything we are doing. If you remember the old fable, the turtle finished before the hare in the race. Start slowly, implementing an idea or two at a time, rather than throwing out everything you are doing and starting over. Begin with two tiers one day each week, then increase them over time. Regular progress is the goal.

> ### *Quotes to Encourage You*
>
> "Never discourage anyone who continually makes progress, no matter how slow . . . even if that someone is yourself!"
>
> —Plato
>
> "No matter how many mistakes you make or how slow you progress, you are still way ahead of everyone who isn't trying."
>
> —Tony Robbins
>
> "Far away there in the sunshine are my highest aspirations. I may not reach them, but I can look up and see their beauty, believe in them, and try to follow where they lead."
>
> —Louisa May Alcott
>
> "I'm a slow walker, but I never walk back."
>
> —Abraham Lincoln
>
> "Painting is a slow process; it takes time to get there, you learn little by little and always want the next painting to be better than the last. For me, success is about this, seeing the slow progress in my work."
>
> —Ali Banisadr
>
> "We may encounter many defeats but we must not be defeated."
>
> —Maya Angelou

Strategy 7: Keep balance in your life. As you are creating a rigorous, differentiated classroom, you will likely become overwhelmed, tired, and discouraged at times. If you want to make a difference with your students, don't work so much that you don't have time for yourself and your family. Set a time to leave at the end of the day, and stick to it, unless there is an emergency. If you need to take work home at night or on the weekend, set a limit of how long you will work. Do your job effectively, but make time for yourself.

Websites That Provide Tips for Work-Life Balance

www.weareteachers.com/best-of-teacher-helpline-9-tips-for-balancing-work-and-family/

www.theguardian.com/teacher-network/teacher-blog/2013/jun/25/teacher-work-life-balance-stress-tips

www.theeducator.com/blog/teacher-work-life-balance-5-tips-for-how-to-have-a-life/

https://education.cu-portland.edu/blog/classroom-resources/five-tips-for-teacher-work-life-balance/

https://pernillesripp.com/2016/01/18/12-ways-i-got-my-life-back-in-balance-as-a-teacher/

www.teachervision.com/blog/morning-announcements/achieving-work-life-balance

www.maneuveringthemiddle.com/work-life-balance-teachers/

What About Homework?

Homework is a part of most of today's classrooms and should be considered in a discussion of scaffolding. Struggling students have particular challenges with homework. For example, we typically assign homework in order to extend learning beyond the classroom. But, if a students doesn't understand the material from class, homework isn't productive. In fact, it is counterproductive.

What does this mean to us? Homework can be effective, but we must plan for its use. Cathy Vatterot, in her book *Rethinking Homework: Best Practices that Support Diverse Needs*, provides some guiding principles as we plan for homework.

> **Principles for Assigning Homework**
>
> Homework should be clearly connected to student learning.
>
> Skills require practice.
>
> More time on task enhances learning.
>
> The quality is as important as the amount of time needed to complete the work.
>
> Children differ in motivation, persistence, and organizational skills and this impacts homework.
>
> Frustration is detrimental to motivation and desire to learn.

An important action for teachers is to set the purpose of homework for students. Cathy suggests sample statements to use with younger and older students.

Sample Statements on the Purpose of Homework	
Younger Students	*Older Students*
The reason for today's homework is . . . ♦ so you can practice doing something you learned in school ♦ so I can find out if you understand what you learned today ♦ to show you something we will learn about soon	The reason for today's homework is to . . . ♦ allow you to apply something you have learned to a new situation ♦ allow you to pull together several things you have already learned ♦ allow you to analyze something you have already learned

You'll also want to be careful with the amount of homework assigned. For struggling students, less is more, and quality is always more important than quantity.

How Can I Partner Effectively With Parents of Struggling Students?

Effective scaffolding moves beyond the classroom. Partnering with the parents and families of your students provides advantages to you, your students, and to their families. Families will have a better idea of what's happening in school, which also allows them to help support their son or daughter at home. Students benefit when they receive encouragement at home. And teachers benefit when learning is reinforced and supported by parents and families. Let's discuss how to PAIR with parents and families to improve student learning. Please note that I'll be using the word "parents," but consider it all-inclusive with families.

> **PAIR With Parents**
> Partnerships are a two-way street
> Accentuate the positive
> Inform and transform
> Relationships are shared

Partnerships Are a Two-Way Street

A true partnership is more than communication from school to home. Although it's our responsibility to take the initiative to form partnerships, everyone has a role. I've found that most parents are willing to help, but they need specific ways to help.

Kendra, the former teacher from earlier chapters, sends home an interactive newsletter every two weeks. Besides the information, there is a question for the parents to answer and send back. She has a high return rate because students receive points for returning the newsletter. She also uses interactive homework.

> For example, I'll take a picture of something my students did in school. Then, I write "Ask me what I learned today" at the top of the page. The parents have to write what their son or daughter said. This lets me know if the students even remember what happened. I'm also always about getting feedback on my own performance and when the parent writes a reflection on what their child is learning, it gives you insight on how well you taught.

It's also helpful to provide parents a list of ways they can help at home. This should include clear guidelines of what constitutes appropriate help.

> **General Tips for Parents**
>
> Encourage your son or daughter to give 100% at all times.
>
> Reinforce concepts and habits the teacher is trying to build. If Jonathan is learning how to multiply percents at school, have him help you calculate the tip at a restaurant.
>
> Encourage your son or daughter to set a designated time when homework will be completed every day.
>
> Provide a quiet, well-lit environment at home with all of the materials necessary for completing school tasks (extra paper, scissors, pens, pencils, pencil sharpener, a dictionary, markers, highlighters, a ruler, calculator, index cards, etc.).
>
> Prevent brain freeze—allow your son or daughter to take a short break every 30 minutes or between homework tasks.
>
> Be careful not to give answers to homework questions; instead, offer advice about where to look for an answer.
>
> Model what productive work looks like. When your son or daughter does homework, you do yours too (balance a checkbook, pay the bills, etc.).

Accentuate the Positive

I called every parent during the first month of school to introduce myself and tell them something positive about their son or daughter. I thought of parent relationships like a bank; I needed to make a deposit before I made a withdrawal. This is particularly true of parents of struggling students. I didn't want my first phone call to be the one about a poor grade or a discipline problem. One time, it took 17 calls to reach a parent before I was finally successful. It took about 5 minutes to convince her I wasn't calling because Marcus was in trouble. She finally said she had never received a call from a teacher telling her something positive about her son. She thanked me and immediately offered her help anytime I needed it. Five weeks later, when Marcus was in trouble in class, she supported me 100%. Focusing on the positive has benefits for you, your students, and their parents.

Ways to Share Positive News Through Social Media

There are many social media tools you can use to communicate with parents and to share positive news. As a caution, be sure you are protecting the privacy of your classroom and your students. For example, on Pinterest, don't name your boards with your location or your full name. Also, there are private blogs that require invitations or membership so you can control who sees the information.

Social Media Tools for Sharing Positive News

Pinterest to share samples of student work (code or remove names for privacy; do not post grades).

Facebook, NextDoor, or a blog to share descriptions of the positive things going on in your classroom.

TikTok to share videos of class activities and presentations (remember to get permission for recording).

Inform and Transform

When I talk to parents, many of them feel as though there is a hidden code in schools—a code they don't understand. Margo and her son moved to a new area when Jared started middle school. She missed the first parent-teacher meeting because she was working. She called the school and left several messages, asking to meet with his teachers, but didn't receive a return call. Margo was frustrated when she told me her story. Another teacher at the school was in one of my classes, so I talked with her. I discovered that the school had a policy that all appointments with teachers were scheduled with the attendance secretary, so the entire teaching team could meet with parents without scheduling conflicts. My graduate student said the principal always explained the policy at the first meeting. So, of course, Margo didn't know because she wasn't at the meeting, and she thought the teachers were just ignoring her. One phone call later, she connected with the teachers, and she and Jared finished the year successfully.

Tip Sheet

Earlier, I shared a set of general guidelines for teachers to provide parents. Another option is to give parents a specific tip sheet for struggling learners.

> **Tips to Help Your Son or Daughter When He/She Is Struggling**
> - It's okay when your son or daughter struggles; it just means they are learning something new.
> - Be positive and encouraging. Use phrases like "you can do it," "I can tell you are moving forward," or "Your effort is paying off."
> - Don't answer questions for your child. Rather, ask them questions to help them figure it out.
> - If they ask you if they are right, ask them what they think. Then ask them to explain why they think they are right or wrong. If you answer for them, you are letting them off the hook for learning.
> - Focus on progress. You might even track it using a chart or stickers.
> - Communicate regularly with your son's or daughter's teacher(s). This will help you understand what is going on and how you can help.

Relationships Are Shared

Many partnerships are destroyed before they start because the teacher believes it is someone else's responsibility to prompt a connection. This was exactly the attitude of my former colleague. If you believe it's the parents' responsibility to communicate and/or follow up with you, that attitude comes through when you talk with them. Communicating with parents is not an extra job; it is part of your job. There is no way you can truly help your students be successful without the support of their parents. And it's up to you to take the first step. Suzanne Okey, a former teacher of students with special needs, points out that sometimes PTA meetings and phone calls are not enough.

> In terms of families, I'm big on home visits. I feel like it's always fair to get off your turf and go into the environment where they are most comfortable. It says this is a two way street; I'm not expecting you to make all the accommodations; I'll meet you where you are. If teachers truly want to form partnerships, they cannot expect it all to be "come to me;" you have to be willing to go to them. Sometimes I sent a letter. It is important to give them options, such as meeting them in neutral places (the public library or McDonald's) in order to preserve their privacy and dignity. Not everyone has transportation or telephones, and they don't want to advertise that to world.

It's our responsibility to connect with parents; the benefits outweigh any challenges.

Key Ideas

- Creating an environment in which your students are intrinsically motivated will benefit their overall learning.
- You will always have too much to do. Work with others to manage your list.
- Provide quality homework so it isn't a stumbling block for your struggling learners.
- Create partnerships with parents of your students in order to provide them the best support.

Thoughts to Consider

1. What are two or three main points you learned?
2. What is one strategy you would like to implement?
3. What is a question you would like to explore in more depth?

Bibliography

Allen, J. (2004). *Tools for teaching content literacy*. Portland, ME: Stenhouse.

Allen, J. (2008). *More tools for teaching content literacy*. Portland, ME: Stenhouse.

Allen, J. (2014). *Tools for teaching academic vocabulary*. Portland, ME: Stenhouse.

Archer, A. L., & Hughes, C. A. (2011). *Explicit instruction: Effective and efficient teaching*. New York: Guilford Press.

Arechiga, D. (2012). *Reaching English language learners in every classroom*. New York: Routledge.

Armstrong, T. (2012). *Neurodiversity in the classroom*. Alexandria, VA: Association for Supervision and Curriculum Development.

Bailey, F., & Pransky, K. (2014). *Memory at work in the classroom*. Alexandria, VA: Association for Supervision and Curriculum Development.

Beachboard, C., & Dause, M. (2020). *10 keys to student empowerment*. New York: Routledge.

Beck, I. L., McKeown, M. G., & Kucan, L. (2008). *Creating robust vocabulary*. New York: Guilford Press.

Blackburn, B. R. (2016). *Motivating struggling learners: Ten strategies for student success*. New York: Routledge.

Blackburn, B. R. (2017). *Rigor and assessment in the classroom*. New York: Routledge.

Blackburn, B. R. (2018). *Rigor is not a four-letter word* (3rd ed.). New York: Routledge.

Blackburn, B. R. (2019). *Rigor and differentiation in the classroom*. New York: Routledge.

Blackburn, B. R. (2020). *Rigor in the remote learning classroom*. New York: Routledge.

Blackburn, B. R. (2021a). *Rigor for students with special needs* (2nd ed.) New York: Routledge.

Blackburn, B. R. (2021b). *Rigor in the remote learning classroom*. New York: Routledge.

Blackburn, B. R. (2021c). *Rigor in your classroom: A toolkit for teachers* (2nd ed.). New York: Routledge.

Blackburn, B. R., & Armstrong, A. (2019). *Rigor in the 6–12 math and science classroom*. New York: Routledge.

Blackburn, B. R., & Armstrong, A. (2020). *Rigor in the K-5 math and science classroom*. New York: Routledge.
Blackburn, B. R., Armstrong, A., & Miles, M. (2018). Using writing to spark learning in math, science, and social studies. *ASCD Express, 13*(16). Retrieved from www.ascd.org/ascd-express/vol13/1316-blackburn. aspx?utm_source=ascdexpress&utm_medium=email&utm_ campaign=Express%2D13%2D16
Blackburn, B. R., & Miles, M. (2019). *Rigor in the 6–12 language arts and social studies classroom*. New York: Routledge.
Blackburn, B. R., & Miles, M. (2020). *Rigor in the K-5 language arts and social studies classroom*. New York: Routledge.
Blackburn, B. R., & Witzel, B. (2018). *Rigor in the RTI/MTSS classroom*. New York: Routledge.
Blackburn, B. R., & Witzel, B. (2021). *Rigor for students with special needs* (2nd ed.). New York: Routledge.
Bull, G., & Bull, L. (Eds.). (2010). *Teaching with digital video*. Arlington, VA: International Society for Technology Education.
Burns, N. (2023). *Inspiring deep learning with metacognition*. Thousand Oaks, CA: Corwin Press.
Causton, J., & Macleod, K. (2020). *From behaving to belonging*. Alexandria, VA: Association for Supervision and Curriculum Development.
Chandler, A. (2022). *The flexible SEL classroom* (2nd ed.). New York: Routledge.
Cleveland, K. P. (2011). *Teaching boys who struggle in school*. Alexandria, VA: Association for Supervision and Curriculum Development.
Conklin, W. (2006). *Instructional strategies for diverse learners*. Huntington Beach, CA: Shell Education.
Cummins, S. (2013). *Close reading of informational texts*. New York: Guilford Press.
Davis, K. A., Zorwick, M. L. W., Roland, J., & Wade, M. M. (2016). *Using debate in the classroom*. New York: Routledge.
DeBono, E. (1999). *Six thinking hats*. New York, NY: Little, Brown and Company.
Diller, D. (2005). *Practice with purpose*. Portland, ME: Stenhouse.
Dimich, N., Erkens, C., & Schimmer, T. (2022). *Jackpot! Nurturing student investment through assessment*. Bloomington, IN: Solution Tree.
Echevarria, J., Frey, N., & Fisher, D. (2016). *How to reach the hard to teach*. Alexandria, VA: Association for Supervision and Curriculum Development.
Erdmann, B., Wood, S. M., Gobble, T., & Marzano, R. J. (2023). *The new art of science of teaching science*. Bloomington, IN: Solution Tree.
Ferlazzo, L. (2013). *Self-driven learning: Teaching strategies for student motivation*. New York: Routledge.

Ferlazzo, L., & Sypnieski, K. H. (2018). *The ELL teacher's toolbox*. San Francisco, CA: Jossey-Bass.

Fisher, D., & Frey, N. (2015). *Text-dependent questions*. Thousand Oaks, CA: Corwin.

Fisher, D., & Frey, N. (2016). *Gradual release of responsibility in the classroom*. Alexandria, VA: Association for Supervision and Curriculum Development.

Fisher, D., Frey, N., & Hit, S. A. (2016). *Intentional and targeted teaching*. Alexandria, VA: Association for Supervision and Curriculum Development.

Fisher, D., Frey, N., & Pumpian, I. (2012). *How to create a culture of achievement*. Alexandria, VA: Association for Supervision and Curriculum Development.

Fisher, D., Frey, N., Ortega, S., & Hattie, J. (2023). *Teaching students to drive their learning*. Thousand Oaks, CA: Corwin Press.

Fisher, D., Frey, N., & Rothenberg, C. (2008). *Content-area conversations*. Alexandria, VA: Association for Supervision and Curriculum Development.

Fogelberg, E., Skaalinder, C., Satz, P., Hiller, B., Bernstein, L., & Vitantonio, S. (2008). *Integrating literacy and math*. New York: Guilford Press.

Frey, N., Fisher, D., & Almarode, J. (2023). *How scaffolding works*. Thousand Oaks, CA: Corwin Press.

Frey, N., Fisher, D., & Smith, D. (2022). *The social-emotional learning playbook*. Thousaand Oaks, CA: Corwin Press.

Fulwiler, B. R. (2007). *Writing in science: How to scaffold instruction to support learning*. Portsmouth, NH: Heinemann.

Garner, B. K. (2007). *Getting to got it*. Alexandria, VA: Association for Supervision and Curriculum Development.

Gibbons, P. (2009). *English learners academic literacy and thinking: Learning in the challenge zone*. Portsmouth, NH: Heinemann.

Gibbons, P. (2014). *Scaffolding language, scaffolding learning*. Portsmouth, NH: Heinemann.

Goodwin, B., & Rouleau, K. (2023). *The new classroom instruction that works*. Alexandria, VA: Association for Supervision and Curriculum Development.

Grafwallner, P. (2020). *Ready to learn*. Bloomington, IN: Solution Tree.

Grafwallner, P. (2021). *Not yet . . . and that's ok: How productive struggle fosters student learning*. Bloomington, IN: Solution Tree.

Grafwallner, P. (2023). *Clearing the path for developing learners*. Bloomington, IN: Solution Tree.

Hale, E. (2022). *High attention reading*. New York: Teachers College Press.

Hall, S. L. (2018). *10 success factors for literacy intervention: Getting results with MTSS in elementary schools*. Alexandria, VA: Association for Supervision and Curriculum Development.

Harmon, J. M., Wood, K. D., & Hedrick, W. B. (2006). *Instructional strategies for teaching content vocabulary*. Westerville, OH: National Middle School Association.

Hattie, J., Fisher, D., & Frey, N. (2017). *Visible learning for mathematics*. Thousand Oaks, CA: Corwin Press.

Hattie, J., Fisher, D., Frey, N., & Clarke, S. (2021). *Collective student efficacy*. Thousand Oaks, CA: Corwin Press.

Hattie, J., & Zierer, K. (2018). *10 Mindframes for visible learning*. New York: Routledge.

Haynes, J. (2007). *Getting started with English language learners*. Alexandria, VA: Association for Supervision and Curriculum Development.

Herrell, A., & Jordan, M. (2004). *Fifty strategies for teaching English language learners* (2nd ed.). Upper Saddle River, NJ: Pearson, Merrill, Prentice Hall.

Hess, K. (2023). *Rigor by design, not chance*. Alexandria, VA: Association for Supervision and Curriculum Development.

Hill, J. D., & Flynn, K. M. (2006). *Classroom instruction that works with English language learners*. Alexandria, VA: Association for Supervision and Curriculum Development.

Jenkins, M. C., & Murawski, W. W. (2024). *Connecting high-leverage practices to student success: Collaboration in inclusive classrooms*. Thousand Oaks, CA: Corwin Press.

Jensen, E. (2013). *Engaging students with poverty in mind: Practical strategies for raising achievement*. Alexandria, VA: Association of Supervision and Curriculum Development.

Jensen, E. (2019). *Poor students, rich teaching*. Bloomington, IN: Solution Tree.

Jensen, E. (2022). *Teaching with poverty and equity in mind*. Alexandria, VA: Association for Supervision and Curriculum Development.

Jolly, A. (2016). *STEM by design*. New York: Routledge.

Koenig, R. (2010). *Learning for keeps: Teaching the strategies essential for creating independent learners*. Alexandria, VA: Association of Supervision and Curriculum Development.

Kramer, S. V., & Schuhll, S. (2023). *Acceleration for all*. Bloomington, IN: Solution Tree.

Lavoie, R. (2007). *The motivation breakthrough: Six secrets to turning on the tuned-out child*. New York: Touchstone.

Linder, R. (2013). *The common core guidebook: Informational text lessons 6–8*. Atlanta: The Literacy Initiative.

Mabry, T. (2022). *Perspective! The secret to student motivation and success*. Thousand Oaks, CA: Corwin Press.

Marzano, J., & Simms, J. A. (2014). *Questioning sequences in the classroom*. Bloomington, IN: Marzano Research Laboratory.

Marzano, R. J., Pickering, D. J., with Heflebower, T. (2011). *The highly engaged classroom*. Bloomington, IN: Marzano Resources.

Marzano, R. J., Pickering, D. J., & Pollock, J. E. (2001). *Classroom instruction that works*. Alexandria, VA: Association for Supervision and Curriculum Development.

McCain, T. (2021). *Problems-first learning*. Bloomington, IN: Solution Tree.

McEwan-Adkins, E. K. (2010). *40 reading intervention strategies for K-6 students*. Bloomington, IN: Solution Tree.

McEwan-Adkins, E. K. (2016). *The 7 thinking hats of skilled readers*. West Palm Beach, FL: Learning Sciences International.

McHugh, M. L. (2023). *Bringing project-based learning to life in mathematics*. Thousand Oaks, CA: Corwin Press.

McKinney, R., & Urlik, C. (2023). *Accelerating learning for all*. Thousand Oaks, CA: Corwin Press.

McTighe, J. (2017). *Designing and using essential questions*. Alexandria, VA: Association for Supervision and Curriculum Development.

Mendler, A. N. (2012). *Motivating students who don't care* (2nd ed.). Bloomington, IN: Solution Tree Press.

Mendler, A. N., & Mendler, B. D. (2019). *Motivating and managing student behavior with dignity*. Alexandria, VA: Association for Supervision and Curriculum Development.

Murray-Darden, S., & Turner, G. Y. (2023). *Serving educational equity*. Thousand Oaks, CA: Corwin Press.

Neuen, S., & Tebeaux, E. (2018). *Writing science right*. New York: Routledge.

Newman, D. (2020). *The noisy classroom*. New York: Routledge.

Olson, C. B., Balius, A., McCourtney, E., & Widtmann, M. (2018). *Thinking tools for your readers and writers*. New York: Teachers College Press.

Parrish, N. (2022). *The independent learner*. Bloomington, IN: Solution Tree.

Pearsall, F. (2023). *Classroom dynamics*. Bloomington, IN: Solution Tree.

Pike, K., & Mumper, J. (2004). *Making nonfiction and other informational texts come alive*. Boston, MA: Pearson Allyn and Bacon.

Pinto, L. E., Spares, S., & Driscoll, L. (2012). *95 strategies for remodeling instruction*. Thousand Oaks, CA: Corwin.

Quaglia, R., & Fox, K. (2019). *Fostering student voice*. Alexandria, VA: Association for Supervision and Curriculum Development.

Rollins, S. P. (2004). *Learning in the fast lane*. Alexandria, VA: Association for Supervision and Curriculum Development.

Rothstein, D., & Santana, L. (2011). *Make just one change*. Cambridge, MA: Harvard Education Press.

Sangiovanni, J. J., Katt, S., & Dykema, K. J. (2020). *Productive math struggle*. Thousand Oaks, CA: Corwin.

Santa, C., Havens, L., & Macumber, E. (1996). *Creating independence through student-owned strategies*. Dubuque, IA: Kendall/Hunt.

Saunders, E. (2023). *Stick the learning*. Bloomington, IN: Solution Tree.

Schmidt, P. S., & Kruger-Ross, M. J. (2022). *Reimagining literacies in the digital age*. St. Louis, MO: National Council of Teachers of English.

Schmidt, R. A., & Marzano, R. J. (2015). *Recording and representing knowledge*. West Palm Beach, FL: Learning Sciences International.

Schmoker, M. (2023). *Results now 2.0*. Alexandria, VA: Association for Supervision and Curriculum Development.

Seale, C. (2020). *Thinking like a lawyer: A framework for teaching critical thinking to all students*. New York: Routledge.

Shirley, D., & Hargreaves, A. (2021). *Five paths of student engagement*. Thousand Oaks, CA: Solution Tree.

Silver, H. F., & Perini, M. J. (2010). *The interactive lecture*. Alexandria, VA: Association for Supervision and Curriculum Development.

Silver, H. F., Strong, R. W., & Perini, M. (2000). *Discovering nonfiction*. Santa Monica, CA: Canter and Associates, Inc.

Small, M. (2009). *Good questions, great ways to differentiate mathematics instruction*. New York: Teachers College Press.

Smith, D., Frey, N., Fisher, D., & Jung, L. A. (2020). *Better behavior practices*. Alexandria, VA: Association for Supervision and Curriculum Development.

Smith, D., Frey, N., Pumpian, I., & Fisher, D. (2017). *Building equity*. Alexandria, VA: Association for Supervision and Curriculum Development.

Smith, M. W., Wilhelm, J. D., & Fredricksen, J. E. (2012). *Oh, yeah?!* Portsmouth, NH: Heinemann.

Sousa, D., & Tomlinson, C. A. (2010). *Differentiation and the brain*. Alexandria, VA: Association for Supervision and Curriculum Development.

Sprenger, M. (2021). *The essential 25: Teaching the vocabulary that makes or breaks student understanding*. Alexandria, VA: Association for Supervision and Curriculum Development.

Stanley, T. (2020). *Promoting rigor through higher level questioning*. Waco, TX: Prufrock Press Inc.

Strasser, J., & Bresson, L. M. (2017). *Big questions for young minds*. Washington, DC: National Association for the Education of Young Children.

Sturtevant, J. A. (2017). *Hacking engagement again*. Cleveland, OH: Times 10.

Tankersley, K. (2005). *Literacy strategies for grades 4–12*. Alexandria, VA: Association for Supervision and Curriculum Development.

Tomlinson, C. A. (2022). *Everybody's classroom*. New York: Teachers College Press.

Villa, R. A., & Thousand, J. S. (2017). *Leading an inclusive school: Access and success for ALAL students*. Alexandria, VA: Association of Supervision and Curriculum Development.

Walqui, A., & van Lier, L. (2010). *Scaffolding the academic success of adolescent English language learners*. San Francisco, CA: WestEd.

Walsh, J. A. (2022). *Questioning for formative feedback*. Alexandria, VA: Association for Supervision and Curriculum Development.

Walsh, J. A., & Sattes, B. D. (2015). *Questioning for classroom discussion*. Alexandria, VA: Association for Supervision and Curriculum Development.

Weiderhold, C. (1995). *Cooperative learning and higher level thinking: The Q-Matrix*. San Clemente, CA: Kagan.

Wells, J., & Reid, J. (2004). *Writing anchors*. Portland, ME: Stenhouse Publishers.

Wiggins, A. (2017). *The best class you never taught*. Alexandria, VA: Association for Supervision and Curriculum Development.

Wilhelm, J. (2002). *Action strategies for deepening comprehension*. New York: Scholastic.

Williamson, R., & Blackburn, B. (2019). *Rigor in your school: A toolkit for leaders* (2nd ed.). New York: Routledge.

Williamson, R., & Blackburn, B. (2020). *7 strategies for improving your school*. New York: Routledge.

Wilson, D., & Conyers, M. (2020). *Developing growth mindsets*. Alexandria, VA: Association for Supervision and Curriculum Development.

Wolsey, T. D., & Lapp, D. (2017). *Literacy in the disciplines*. New York: Guilford Press.

Wood, K. D., Lapp, D., Flood, J., & Taylor, D. B. (2008). *Guiding readers through text* (2nd ed.). Newark, DE: International Reading Association.

Wormeli, R. (2005). *Summarization in any subject*. Alexandria, VA: Association for Supervision and Curriculum Development.

Zwiers, J., & Crawford, M. (2011). *Academic conversations*. Portsmouth, NH: Stenhouse.

For Product Safety Concerns and Information please contact our EU
representative GPSR@taylorandfrancis.com
Taylor & Francis Verlag GmbH, Kaufingerstraße 24, 80331 München, Germany